Copyright © 2023 by Peter Bradford

All rights reserved. No part of this publication may be reproduced without written permission from the publisher or author except as permitted by U.S. copyright law.

979-8-9895455-0-6 (Paperback)
979-8-9895455-1-3 (Paperback)

Imprint: Bee Better Movement

This is a work of creative non-fiction. All the events in this memoir are true to the best of the author's memory. All the names and identifying features have been changed to protect the identity of certain parties. The author does not represent any company, corporation, or brand mentioned herein. The views expressed in this memoir are solely those of the author. The advice and strategies contained herein may not be suitable for your situation. You should consult with a professional when appropriate. Neither the publisher nor the author shall be liable for any loss of profit or other commercial damages, including but not limited to special, incidental, consequential, personal, or other damages.

Book Cover by: Sarah Larnarch
First Printing Edition

# Table of Contents

Acknowledgments ................................................. 8

Preface ................................................................... 9

Introduction ....................................................... 11

Why Beeing Good isn't Good For You ............. 13

    What's the Alternative? ................................. 15

    Breaking The Habit ....................................... 17

    The Dangers of Saying Good ........................ 18

        It Keeps You Average ................................ 18

        It Leaves No Room for Reflection ........... 20

        It Limits Your Ideas .................................. 22

        Mediocrity is Fatal .................................... 23

        It Lacks Enthusiasm ................................. 23

        It Doesn't Differentiate ............................. 25

    Ingredient for Propulsion ............................. 29

    Rock Bottom isn't a Life Sentence ............... 33

    Escaping Rock Bottom .................................. 36

        Negative Patterns and Behaviors .............. 36

        So, I decided to make it a game. ............. 36

        I took it a step further. ............................. 36

        Negative People ........................................ 37

    The Shift: Victimhood to Empowerment ........ 40

- Extract Value from Your Situation ........................ 43
- Stay Positive in Challenging Times ........................ 46
- Using Rock Bottom for Self-Reflection .................... 49

Fear, False Starts, and Doubts ................................... 51
- Understanding Fear .................................................. 53
- Appropriate and Disproportionate Fear ................... 56
- Impact of Fear on Decision-Making ......................... 58
- Recognizing False Starts .......................................... 59
- Reasons Behind False Starts .................................... 61
  - Lack of Clarity ...................................................... 61
  - Feeling Overwhelmed ........................................... 61
  - Shifting Priorities ................................................. 63
- Allowing False Starts ............................................... 64
  - Self-Doubt ............................................................ 64
  - Self-Sabotage ........................................................ 64
- Jumping Over Doubts ............................................. 65
  - Recognizing Self-doubt ........................................ 67
  - Be More Mindful ................................................. 67
  - Embrace Self-Compassion ................................... 68
- Piercing Through Doubt ......................................... 68
  - Embrace Failure as Learning ................................ 69
  - Celebrate Your Successes ..................................... 70

- Surround Yourself with Positivity .......................... 70
- Take Action Despite Doubts ................................ 71
- Embracing Fear, False Starts, and Doubts ................ 72
- Changing Inside, Design Your Own Life .................. 75
- Understanding the Power of Internal Change .......... 77
- The Power of Visualization ........................................ 78
- The Power of Affirmation .......................................... 79
  - Visualize Your Goal: ............................................... 80
  - Choose Positive Language: ..................................... 80
  - Make it Personal: .................................................... 80
  - Use Empowering Words: ........................................ 81
- Unleashing Your Potential ......................................... 82
- Shifting Your Mindset ................................................ 83
- The Power of an Open Mindset ................................ 84
- How to Effectively Shift Your Mindset ..................... 87
  - Be Aware of Your Current Mindset: ...................... 87
  - Challenge Negative Thoughts: ............................... 87
  - Replace with Positivity: .......................................... 87
  - Practice Gratitude: .................................................. 88
  - Change Your Environment: ................................... 88
- Designing Your Life .................................................... 88
- Changing The Outside, Fake It Till You Make It ..... 90

Why Fake It Till You Make it ...................................... 92

Overcoming Limiting Beliefs ........................................ 94

Adapting to Change ...................................................... 95

Creating a New Habit .................................................. 97

What Can You Do Differently Today? ....................... 99

Body Language ........................................................... 100

Vocabulary .................................................................. 102

Balancing Authenticity .............................................. 105

Embracing External Change ..................................... 106

A Little Gratitude Goes A Long Way ........................... 108

Gratitude and Attitude .............................................. 113

Gratitude and Abundance ......................................... 115

Gratitude and Relationships ..................................... 119

Gratitude and Challenges ......................................... 125

How to Remain Grateful ........................................... 125

    Stay in the Present: ............................................... 126

    Wear Rose-Colored Glasses: ................................ 126

    Embrace Self-Growth: .......................................... 127

    Rediscover Your Childlike Wonder: .................... 127

    Get a Journal: ........................................................ 128

People and Situations Change, Feeding off Your Positivity ................................................................................. 130

| | |
|---|---|
| The Dynamics of Change | 132 |
| Navigating Change with Positivity | 135 |
| Stay Positive in the Face of Change | 137 |
|    Envision a Brighter Future: | 137 |
|    Prioritize Self-Care: | 138 |
|    Turn off Your Gadgets: | 139 |
|    Check Your Language: | 141 |
|    Start the Day on a Great Note: | 144 |
| Meet Other "Great" People | 145 |
| The Unwavering Power of Positivity | 147 |
| Changing One Word to BeeBetter | 148 |
| Self-Reflection | 152 |
| Setting Clear Goals | 152 |
| Upgrading Language | 153 |
| Taking Consistent Action | 155 |
| Overcoming Challenges | 156 |
| Cultivating Resilience | 160 |
|    Focus on the calmest part of your body. | 161 |
|    Set boundaries and manage your energy wisely. | 161 |
|    Self-soothe through affirmations. | 162 |
|    Journal from the perspective of your stress. | 162 |
|    Journal from the perspective of your calm. | 162 |

    Create compassionate imagery. ........................... 163

    Increase bodily awareness. ................................... 163

    Slow down to six breaths a minute. ................... 164

    Play around with your body language. ............... 164

    Establish a mindful movement practice. ............ 164

    Dance. ...................................................................... 165

    Visualize a future calm self. ................................. 165

    Imagine your mind in slow motion. .................... 165

    Laugh (even if it's forced). ................................... 165

    Try chanting or singing meditation. ................... 166

  Celebrating Progress .................................................. 166

  Living the "Great" Life .............................................. 167

Life is a Journey, not a Destination ............................. 168

  The Power of Learning from Struggles ................... 170

  Early Struggles ........................................................... 173

  Nurturing Relationships and Experiences .............. 177

    Cultivating Genuine Bonds ................................. 181

    The Happiness of Pursuing Passion ................... 182

  The Unending Triumph ............................................ 184

Power of Transformation ............................................... 185

  Purpose and Meaning ............................................... 187

  Discovering Purpose Through Transformation ...... 188

Our Words & Relationships .................................. 190

Transformation and Growth .................................. 192

Final Ode .................................................................. 194

## Acknowledgments

I want to thank the special people who agreed to be included in this book:

To my wife – thank you for finding me, after years of being together you still knock me sideways.

To my mom – you were one of my inspirations for this book thank you for being my mom.

To my little monkey, give me three names… and you already know the rest.

To my dad – thank you for all the adventures, see you on the fairways!

My dog, for not eating the manuscripts and of course my cat for (begrudgingly) for not conniving with the dog to eat the manuscripts.

My deepest thanks go out to Tide for being a happy camper while we edited the manuscripts.

To Lynette – thank you for helping me write this book – always be buzzing!

To Wendy – to the endless phone calls that took hours long just to get my point across. Thank You…

To my loaded gun – keep your aim true and your sights straight… We have more adventures to come!

To my amazing friends, the not-so-amazing ones, and the ones I haven't met yet –

Hello and Thank you…

## Preface

I was in my early 20s when a single conversation with Jean, one of my first bosses, changed my life forever. "How are you?" he had asked, to which I replied, "Good," the standard reply many of us are familiar with.

Rather than acknowledge my generic greeting, he said, "What would it take to be great?" That sentence transformed my life as I shifted from "good" to "great." From that point forward, whenever someone inquired about my well-being, I was "great!" Slowly, I started to adopt a more positive attitude, leading to better outcomes.

After hearing my stories, my daughter, Emma, chose the path of positivity as a teenager, and as she grew older, she realized the value of what I had taught her. Seeing how much better such a simple change had made her life, I knew I had to get the word out there.

When I introduced the concept of the power of one word to my good friend and co-author Lynette, she loved it. In her excitement, she resonated with the word 'buzzing' and soon came to experience the transformation I'd had over two decades ago- a drastic improvement in her life quality. Many struggle to make ends meet in today's fast-paced world, sustain our relationships, and remain relevant. That's why now more than ever, One Word to Bee Better is a life-changing resource that people of all ages, all around the world, need.

This simple but often overlooked habit can help you deal with setbacks, improve the quality of your personal and professional relationships, and change your life. I owe a lot of my happiness to friends and business associates, and for that reason, I am proud to be able to share some of their brilliance and stories with you in this book. Please share your success stories after using your buzzword for 30 days at #buzzwordtobeebetter, #onewordtobeebetter, and #beebettermovement.

## Introduction

Observing people has always held a particular fascination for me. Growing up in a family that embraced constant relocation, I quickly learned the art of adapting to new environments. This skill became invaluable as I navigated through life, whether handling demanding customers during my first job at McDonald's or seeking potential business partners in marketing. Their body language often gave me insights—did they welcome conversation, was small talk necessary, or should I maintain a respectful distance? Early on, I grasped a fundamental truth: the key to gaining others' support, cooperation, or acceptance rested in their happiness.

As the years passed, I made an intriguing discovery: many of us continuously pursue an elusive future of happiness. We continually strive for more wealth, weight loss, or that next rung on the career ladder. Yet, when we eventually attain these goals, an unsettling restlessness often settles in. We yearn for something different or grapple with the fear of losing everything. I've found that achieving happiness in the present hinges on self-awareness and careful monitoring of our mindset—and it's simpler than you might think. It can be as straightforward as changing a single word.

Consider this: how often in a day do you hear the question, "How are you?"—and how much thought do you invest in your response? For most of us, it's a reflex, and we reply without much consideration. But what if we pause to ponder whether our response leans toward positivity or negativity? Are we laying the groundwork for an exceptional day or another ordinary struggle?

This book is fantastic because it helps us unlock our power, the power to effect change, starting today. It doesn't matter if you've convinced yourself that you're a lost cause or have spent years striving for self-improvement; we all can make the world a better place—for ourselves and others.

Suppose you desire to revolutionize your life and cultivate a mindset that empowers you to thrive in the present, enhance your well-being, advance your career, and strengthen your family bonds. In that case, it requires only a single word. A radical shift in your language can recalibrate your mind to achieve greatness however you define it.

In the upcoming chapters, I will leverage expert-backed statistics, proven strategies, and personal experiences to demonstrate how altering your choice of words can profoundly influence every crucial facet of your life.

Feel free to draw from this book what resonates with you, and don't hesitate to share.

> "We all can make the world a better place—for ourselves and others…" – Peter Bradford

## Chapter 1

### **Why Beeing Good isn't Good For You**

As far back as I can remember, I've heard the importance of minding how you speak. As a child, my mother cautioned me whenever I spoke ill of someone, using the famous phrase, "If you don't have anything nice to say, don't say anything at all." I grew up watching movies that bleeped out profanities and wondered why certain songs on the radio had their lyrics muffled. Close supervision over what we say and put out to our audience is a constant in our society because we understand that words carry weight and can profoundly impact the people listening. Despite this knowledge, we often tend to be less mindful about what we say to or about ourselves. We often replay negative thoughts or seldom give a second thought to our answers when people ask about our welfare.

When someone asks, "How are you?" We rarely stop to ponder the appropriate reply and often default to the standard response, "I'm good." But what if I told you being good wasn't good for you? Yep, you heard right. Sometimes, "being good" can affect you negatively.

I know you're wondering how, especially since it's one of the first words we learn as children and something you probably say unconsciously daily. But when we constantly repeat this seemingly harmless reply and its close synonyms, we might fall, if not stay in our comfort zone, unconsciously living smaller lives, not waking to wonder if there's a step above where we currently are.

Now, take a moment and reflect on how often you use the word 'good' or its close equivalent, 'fine' when your colleague asks, "How are you?" when your friendly neighbor inquires, "How's your day going?" or when your partner asks, "How are you feeling?"

"Good, thanks," is almost always the automatic reply to these questions, and we often answer without stopping to reflect. It's simply another mindless response as autonomic in our system as breathing. Language is a powerful tool that does more than help us communicate daily. It shapes our thoughts. When a coach gives his team a pep talk, it can spur them to go out and clinch victory at the last minute.

When a manager berates his staff, he can demoralize them, causing the company to suffer by losing valuable input, and when we say, "I'm good," or "I'm fine," (without deliberation) we settle for the status quo.

Knowing how we talk to others and, more importantly, ourselves is crucial; we'd best be more mindful of how we speak. What we say can go a long way in affecting our relationships, careers, and lives. As the famous saying goes, there is power in the tongue. According to a study by the University of California, people who regularly use positive words experience lower stress levels and better overall mental health.

Of course, that's not to dispute the place of planning and hard work. But what you say, especially your inner monologue, can amplify or diminish the steps you take toward success. Our chosen words can make us happier, stronger, and more resilient to adversity.

## What's the Alternative?

Now that we've established that the comfort of "good" can hinder your growth, does that mean you must throw away your entire vocabulary? No. This book isn't about fancy language or complicated mantras. It's about how simple changes can make a huge difference. If you want to live a more inspiring life than just "good," you must choose a word with the same amount of conviction. For me, that was "great." Simply replacing the word "good" with "great" has made an incredible difference in my career, relationships with family and friends, and outlook on life because I made the conscious effort to embody the meaning of great; I worked towards having a great life because of my choice of words.

> "When someone asks, "How are you?" We rarely stop to ponder the appropriate reply and often default to the standard response, "I'm good." –
> Peter Bradford

When you choose "great" instead of "good," you're reframing your mindset. "Great" isn't just a word. It's an attitude. It's like saying, "I want my life to be extraordinary!" Since I uncovered this little-known truth, I've been able to transform my life for the better, and I know you can, too. I've heard countless stories of people, some of whom you know, unknowingly putting this principle into practice and reaping positive, life-changing results. Even less popular people undoubtedly enjoy the benefits of a more optimistic outlook in their daily lives. With compelling evidence supporting the theory that words matter, I've convinced myself to share this message with the world. Your choice of words can make or break you, so to reach your full potential *"To BeeBetter"* you must speak better.

## Breaking The Habit

It's difficult to unlearn an old habit, especially one that has stuck with you for years. For many of us, the habit of saying "good" automatically is something we picked up as children. It's one of the first things we learn when we start speaking. So, naturally, you shouldn't expect to get with the new program overnight. But guess what? It's doable.

Adopting a "great" mindset was a journey that took me years. My newfound conviction wavered during some of my lowest points, and it was hard to remain "great" during challenging times. It was hard to imagine being "great" when I was simply trying to get through the day.

You'll know what I mean if you've had moments that made you question your self-worth or value in life. When we're at rock bottom, we can easily slip into negative thoughts while still automatically saying "good" without much thought. On the other hand, the determination to be "great" requires more thought and self-control, not only with your words but also with your actions.

Whatever you're facing, I'm here to give you a *great* shake. Your words affect your feelings, and you must be mindful of what you say. To break free from the "good" habit, we need to become mindful in our responses. Instead of the autopilot "good," try pausing momentarily and thinking about how you truly feel. Appreciate the little things. The delicious cup of coffee you had in the morning, your cozy home, your children, your friends. Also, ask yourself if you're really doing all you can to bee "great," and if you're not, what steps can you take to get there.

# The Dangers of Saying Good

## It Keeps You Average

My encounter with Jean formed the cast that would mold me into the man I am today. Before that day, I'd never imagined you could be better than good. While I'd always had a positive attitude, I hadn't made concrete plans to do more with my life. I was content coming to work and doing what I needed to finish the day. It was all about earning a paycheck. Now, don't get me wrong, there's nothing wrong with having that mindset. But it does become stagnant after a while.

Although I wasn't trying to be mediocre at my job, I wasn't putting in any effort to be more. Like a bumble bee, I was busy without giving a thought to how to make my honey richer or which other hives were out there. If you're an Apiologist or bee enthusiast, you might already know that honeybees only leave their hives when conditions become unbearable. They settle until a lack of food, weather changes, and other disturbances force them out. So, finding a new place to call home can be challenging when that happens.

Humans are conditioned to think that being busy is a badge we should display and discuss at every opportunity. Think about the last time you used the phrase, "Sorry, I'm too busy," or something similar as an excuse to get out of an event or avoid taking on more responsibility. While it's essential to establish boundaries and not let your boss or family pile on you, do you ever ask yourself if what you're busy with matters or how it fits into your bigger plan? Like bees, when we're busy simply because we ought to be, it requires an external force to facilitate change.

It takes some people losing their jobs to realize they never really liked it and would rather do something else. During my role in IT support, I was busy fixing computers. And I was good at it. Only *good*. With a 9-5, there's no denying that I was busy. Thankfully, it didn't take a life-altering decision by someone in HR to change that mindset. After my conversation with Jean, I Over the next 5 to 7 years, I decided to break out of my comfort zone and hone my skills.

Soon enough, I became the company's software trainer. When I was ready to take on more responsibility, I went on to a sales support role where I worked first-hand in implementing some of the company's newer processes.

There, I realized working a corporate job wasn't for me. I was great at what I did but knew I could improve elsewhere. I'd developed a passion for marketing, and by 2005, I was ready to take a leap of faith. I started creating and building my own companies, which was tough initially, but it got better; I was determined to improve. And as a famous saying by Anton Chekhov goes, *"Man is what he believes."*

Life has so much more to offer than average. It's full of opportunities to be exceptional, shine brightly, and make a real impact. Think about the people you admire the most. They're probably not the ones who settled for "good enough." They're the ones who dared to be great by exploring their potential, and so can you.

## It Leaves No Room for Reflection

Automatically replying with 'good' doesn't allow you to reflect on the seemingly minor things. When you say "I'm fine" out of habit, you miss a chance for self-reflection. Life is a series of moments, each a unique opportunity for growth and gratitude. So the next time someone asks, "How are you?" reflect on your reply. Focus on how you feel.

Remember that seemingly minor things can be a cause for gratitude. Grabbing a warm cup of coffee on your way to work or singing along with your kids while you drive them to school are little things we often take for granted. Tapping into the power of self-reflection can help you realize there are many reasons to feel great, buzzing, excellent, or on cloud 9! If you're a parent, you can take pride in getting to be your child's first role model. Or, if you find yourself in a care home, you could enjoy smelling the roses in the garden.

On one occasion, my good friend Lynette shared a personal experience with me. She was on a flight from Arizona to New York, while everyone was getting impatient waiting for their flight's boarding gate to open, the intercom announced that her flight had been delayed due to bad weather. On hearing the news, one of the passengers beside her, obviously unhappy about the announcement, said, "That sucks." Although Lynette wasn't thrilled at the news either, it didn't put her in a bad mood either.

*"Well, at least when we finally board, we'll be certain we're safe, and that sounds great to me."*

Taken aback by her undeterred positivity, Lynette piqued the stranger's interest. With time to kill, they started a conversation, and he shared with her some of the challenges he'd been through. His first daughter had been born with seven holes in her heart and was given only a few months to live. Despite such a grim prognosis, he'd been able to enlist the help of his friend, a well-known British business magnate, who garnered the support of some of the best surgeons in the UK. After a grueling five-hour surgery with fears and worries, the surgeon and his team completed the life-saving surgery.

This stranger went on to have another daughter, and both girls were healthy teenagers. He expressed his understanding of the fragility of life and was grateful for the experience despite how traumatic it was at the time.

Lynette asked him, *"So if both your daughters are doing fine, isn't every day a great day?"*

He opened his mouth to speak and closed it, unsure what to say. And on his face, Lynette could see him reflecting on what she'd said, just like I had done when Jean said something similar. By the time they boarded the plane, the man was enthusiastic that despite being a couple of hours late, he was going home to his children, which was great. Changing how you think might be challenging, but pausing to appreciate what you've got can help you live in the present and chase the things that matter. When you switch from "good" to "great," you invite mindfulness into your life. You start to notice the little things that bring joy, and like Lynette's fellow passenger, you're less likely to be deterred by minor inconveniences.

Adopting an "I'm great" attitude can make your life more prosperous and fulfilling. Remember gratitude is a great attitude.

**It Limits Your Ideas**

"Good" is safe and familiar, like a well-worn path through a forest. When we default to this reply or way of thinking, we limit our ideas and settle. We resign our faith in the rat race, chasing after money, that next big promotion, or the newest gadget to make us happy.

Like a hamster running on a wheel, we settle for a mediocrity mindset without ever feeling the need to *beebetter*. Imagine if Edison had been content with "good" candles instead of inventing the great light bulb. Life's most significant breakthroughs happen when we dare to explore the unknown, challenge the status quo, and reject the idea of being mediocre.

Habits of mediocre people that you must avoid:

- They lack intention and a sense of purpose.
- They listen to naysayers.
- They have low expectations.
- They seek personal glory over meaning.
- They have little value for time and money.
- They have a poor attitude to learning.
- They are driven by instant gratification.
- They have no sense of urgency or responsibility.
- They seek to be perfect.
- They're quitters.

## Mediocrity is Fatal

You shouldn't settle for it. We are born with unique qualities and skills perfect for tackling our life purpose. Yours might be inventing the next revolutionary technology, developing an innovative solution for your company, or finally discovering how to rekindle the flame with your partner.

As a young guy in IT support, I had to think outside the box when I decided to *BeeBetter*. I realized I could be more helpful and valuable at work by becoming a software trainer. Knowing that I put in the work and moved up the ladder, intending to go beyond "good." When you shift away from being "good" and adopt the attitude of being "great," you embrace the excitement of new ideas and possibilities.

## It Lacks Enthusiasm

Using the word "good" lacks enthusiasm. How often do you feel pumped when you monotonously reply, "fine," when someone asks about your day? Replacing those words with something more upbeat, like "awesome" or "excellent," can generate genuine excitement in you, which can be contagious.

It could spur you to try new things, meet new people, and work your way through a bucket list of all the things you've always wanted to try.

When Pharrell Williams' single, Happy, debuted in 2013, it was sensational and had millions of people tapping their feet and clapping their hands along to the tune. It became the theme song for the famous motion picture Despicable Me 2 and spent 22 weeks in the top 10 US. It was inescapable and contagious because singing a song about being happy made it easy to be exactly that.

Using a word with more enthusiasm can also put things in perspective. It helps you realize time is short, and if you're not enthusiastic about the things you're doing, it might be time for a reset. Instead of spending time on things that won't matter at the end of your life, you should prioritize things that make you happy.

If you need to feel 'great,' 'excellent,' or 'awesome' at what you do, think of something else. The most significant legacy people leave behind when their time is up is that they help others. You can gain so much joy from volunteering or caring for other people.

Live a life where you show up for yourself every day with a mindset that says, this is what I'm about; these are my values, and this is where I will focus my time. If you spend your time with the people who love you while doing the things you love, you'll carve a unique path with no regrets.

Think about it. When you say "great" or "awesome," you can't help but feel a surge of positive energy. That energy propels you to try new things and tackle challenges with a smile. You become the shining star in the night sky, and people can't help but notice you because you stand out differently in a good way. And when your enthusiasm is contagious, it can inspire those around you.

**It Doesn't Differentiate**

Whenever someone asks, "How's your day going?" and I reply with, "Great, and you?" They're instantly puzzled by my enthusiastic answer. It helps me stand out. These people often follow up with questions like, "why?" "how come?" and that has led to some interesting conversations with strangers that went on to become great friends or chance encounters that made my day.

In a world where several studies show our attention span is steadily declining, grabbing someone's interest within the first few seconds of meeting them could mean your next sale, offer letter, or a lifetime connection. When I eventually left the corporate world in 2005 to start my own business, I leaned heavily on my ability to make connections. The subject of standing out keenly reminds me of a convention I attended in Berlin. I was working with my partner, Matthew, to find Facebook media buyers.

Matthew was the technical expert, so with my background in sales, I naturally assumed the opener position. Since we found ourselves at a convention with thousands of vendors all getting pitches from hopeful business owners just like us, I knew I had to start strong. After casing the floor, I instinctively noticed two sharply dressed men and beckoned to my partner as we approached.

*"Hello, I'm Peter,"* I said, stretching my hand out.

"Hello, Peter. How do you do?" One of the men asked as we exchanged handshakes.

*"Great!"* I confidently replied as I watched them briefly exchange curious glances, obviously intrigued by my rare response. With their attention captured, I could launch my pitch on a positive note, and when I got them intrigued, I would let Matthew take over to explain the more technical concepts. By the end of the conversation, they'd established themselves as Facebook media buyers, and we could exchange information. Matthew and I connected with other buyers using this technique, making our Berlin trip successful.

You see, most folks are used to hearing "good" all the time. It's a default they're used to. So when you respond with "great," it catches their attention. In my experience, many people follow up by asking, "Why great?" or "What's so great about it?" Whether out of curiosity or sheer amazement, people usually wonder what the source of my enthusiasm is and for some they want to know if they can tap from it too.

And when you've grabbed their interest, you can sell yourself with more confidence. Of course, not everyone is always intrigued by such an optimistic response, but I've met some of the most wonderful people on Earth by giving a reply that stands out.

Whether at a drive-through, mall, or office event, a unique reply that makes people smile or curious can help you garner more interactions. Nothing is exciting about saying, "I'm fine, thanks," and unless you're talking with family members or friends, your customers, clients, and strangers will unlikely have a memorable impression of you after exchanging pleasantries.

Saying *"good"* might feel safe, but it could also come at the cost of missing out on the breakthrough you desperately want.

To be an outstanding person, you need to have exceptional interactions. Using words like "great" or "fantastic" can be your unique signature that sparks curiosity and makes you more memorable.

*So, how are you today?* Now that you understand the power of language and how automatic replies like "Good," "Fine," and "Not too bad" can keep you average, what are you going to do about it?

Thinking about a more positive reply doesn't necessarily mean lying; it simply requires deeper self-reflection on what you have, what matters, and how you want to feel. It requires a mindset tune-up, commitment, and hard work. But you have what it takes to make a 180-degree turn with your choice of words. So choose another answer and see what happens. In this book, we will provide you with all the tools you need to BeeBetter through the power of changing one word.

I will tell you a secret: successful and happy people have figured out the Power of One Word to BeeBetter - some just haven't realized what they did to turn their lives around. So, how can you choose a better word that helps you reflect more, feel more enthusiastic, and stand out in a crowd? How can you make this new habit stick, especially when you're at rock bottom? I've got you.

Throughout this book, I'll take you through the possible roadblocks you might encounter, like fear and doubt, and how you can remain "great" even at your lowest. I'll show you how a tiny change in how you speak to yourself, and others can lead to a massive transformation in your life.

But it's important to remember that lasting change doesn't come overnight. Still, moving toward your goal of achieving a life that goes beyond "good," a life that is "great," is endlessly better than staying where you are right now.

## Chapter 2

**Rock Bottom: An Ingredient for Propulsion**

I know that remaining positive in adverse circumstances can be a challenge. My divorce was one of the lowest points in my life, and I was in a dark place for a long time. When my ex-wife and I called it quits after 16 years together, 13 of those in marriage, it felt like my family was disappearing.

Despite having joint custody of our then 12-year-old daughter, my ex-wife had decided it would be best for them to move back to Canada, which took a toll on me.

Knowing that I wouldn't be able to be as present as I would've liked in my daughter's life was a bitter pill to swallow. I was rolling in a pool of self-pity for months and would occasionally cry at random times, wondering why me. Why did it feel like the world was working against me?

It hurt to know I wouldn't be there for the small stuff. The breakfasts, trips to the park, the intimate chats, and even casual car rides to school would become a distant memory.

Although I tried my best by splitting time in Canada, facetiming as much as possible, and ensuring prompt child support payments, it felt different. On top of the fear that my family was imploding, business wasn't great. I had recently sold my software company to start a marketing company called Trendy Tactics. True to my passion for helping people, I started the company specifically to specialize in generating traffic for small to medium-sized businesses. It was a risky move, but I had faith in my partners.

However, at the time of my divorce, Trendy Tactics was undergoing an expansion that significantly dipped into my finances as we hired new staff and tried to scale up without toppling like a house of cards.

The situation elevated my stress levels and impacted my physical and mental well-being. Knowing things were beginning to spiral out of control, I sought help. When I finally got around to seeing a health professional, my test results showed my elevated stress levels were wreaking havoc on my hormones. At that point, every area of my life felt like it was going through a total meltdown - my business, my family, and my health. This was not my envisioned life, and I felt like a failure.

In my darkest hour, I remembered my conversation with my former boss, Jean. I'd tried to poke holes in his theory a few days after our encounter precisely because of scenarios like this. Replacing "good" with "great" seemed like a quirky and fun reply, but it was inevitably unfeasible. No one can always be great. At the time, I certainly wasn't. Thankfully, I had an answer when my life seemed to take a nosedive.

Years before I hit rock bottom, I confronted Jean. A few days after our chance encounter, I went to his office to challenge his advice. He'd always had an open-door policy, and I had no qualms telling him he was wrong.

*"What if my whole family dies? I wouldn't be so great then."* I said, convinced I'd found the loophole in his unnecessarily optimistic outlook.

*"That's not true."* He countered. "Peter, you'd still be a great person, even if not on that day or at that time."

His reply stumped me. In those days, my attitude and emotions were dependent on my circumstances. And when I was down on my luck, I was inclined to feel terrible, fearful, and hopeless. Until my divorce, it'd been easy to be better when things were rosy. Suddenly, they weren't anymore, and it was much more challenging, nearly impossible, to feel great.

In hindsight, those events were a turning point for me. Once I realized my life wasn't heading in my desired direction, I knew something had to change.

I might have started by trying to fake it till I made it, but I quickly realized that at any point in time, I could say, "No, I am not going down like this. I am going to do something about this now." For some people, rock bottom is losing their job, coming to terms with the fact they have an addiction, or losing a loved one. It's not always easy to remain positive when grieving, experiencing unfulfillment, or feeling stuck in a toxic cycle. You might even feel a sense of dread as you potentially head downwards. But if you don't accept that despite your circumstances, things can get better, and put in the work to get there, you'll remain in the pit you've dug for yourself.

## Rock Bottom isn't a Life Sentence

When we find ourselves at rock bottom, it can feel as though life has dealt us an insurmountable blow. 25-year-old Yusra Mardini was a member of the Refugee Olympic Athletes when she won the 100-meter butterfly heat race in the 2016 Rio Summer Olympics.

Growing up in Damascus during the Syrian Civil War, the odds were stacked against her. At only 17, her family's home was destroyed in the war, forcing her and her sister to flee the country.

For over a month, they made their way through Europe, eventually having to swim through the tumultuous Aegean Sea when their dinghy stopped working and began taking on water. I can only imagine how much resilience it took to survive such unbearable conditions, barely clinging to life with no food or water and the cold ocean enveloping most of your body like a blanket.

Despite several near-death experiences and harsh conditions, Yusra and her sister made it to Berlin. They'd survived a grueling journey and were happy to settle down in relative harmony. If Yusra had slipped into depression mourning the loss of her family and her home, it would've been perfectly understandable. Life flipping your entire world can diminish any motivation to forge onward.

Yet, Yusra used her unique circumstances to keep going. Before the crisis had torn her out of her home, she'd been a competitive swimmer, representing Syria in the 2012 FINA World Swimming Championship. Despite being a refugee in a foreign country and learning a new language, she was determined to continue her training and found a coach to help her reach her goal of swimming at the Olympics. Yusra achieved that goal less than a year later, and the 2022 Swimmers film commemorated her triumphant story.

Yusra chose not to let her traumatic past stop her from achieving greatness. Instead, she leveraged it as a personal catalyst for transformation. Yes, Yusra must've battled with negative emotions like hopelessness and despair. She might have even considered giving up several times on the harrowing journey from Syria to Berlin. But in the end, she realized that her past didn't have to define her, and if she chose to *bee* "great," she could be. Whether you're having a tough time making something of yourself, at work, or with your family, it's important to remember that rock bottom is not a life sentence.

As the famous Persian adage goes, "This too shall pass." The fact things are rough now doesn't mean they always will be. Besides, with the right attitude, you can use your circumstances as a springboard for a brighter future.

You might not realize it, but you're at a turning point. Every battle starts in your mind, and whenever you're ready, you can rise above rock bottom and *BeeBetter* than you were yesterday.

**scan me.**
Get your free workbook
to help jumpstart your
journey.
#word?

**thank you.**
You can also visit
www.beebettermovement.com
and download the free
workbook from there.

# Escaping Rock Bottom

## Negative Patterns and Behaviors

One of the crucial steps in breaking free from the shackles of rock bottom is recognizing the negative patterns that led you there in the first place. When I started to adopt a "great" attitude, I noticed my negative attitude still held me back. Breaking the habit of grumbling or simply replying with, "Good, thanks," was instinctive. So, I would kick myself often for forgetting that I wasn't just good but "great."

Yes, I understood that when I replied with "great," it boosted my confidence and helped me stand out, but getting the habit to stick was still a challenge. If you've read any article or book on building good habits, you know that making it easy is one of the best ways to adopt a new routine.

**So, I decided to make it a game.**
I began keeping score of how many times I said something mundane like "good," "fine," or "well." It made me mindful of what I said or thought, making me less likely to repeat those negative patterns. But I didn't stop there.

**I took it a step further.**

I told myself I would earn a point whenever I could replace those words with "great," "excellent," or something more enthusiastic. Since I aimed to score more than yesterday, I remained conscious of my word choices daily until my desired reply became instinctive. Another area where people tend to build negative habits is their health. Although we know it's essential, we often ignore experts' nutrition, sleep, and exercise recommendations. We all want to feel happy and fulfilled, but it's hard to do that in a body held back by our negative habits.

Feeling great is much easier when you're physically and mentally fit. We can improve our health by watching what we eat, ensuring enough exercise and rest, and staying away from things we know are detrimental to our bodies. Whatever your bad habit is, like turning the TV on instead of going to the gym, talking down to your kids when you promised you wouldn't, or other self-sabotaging behaviors, honest introspection, and a willingness to confront your shortcomings will help you identify these negative patterns. Once you've acknowledged these destructive habits, you can make conscious decisions to act differently. You can choose more positive ways and behaviors that align with your desired outcome.

## Negative People

When my family moved to Toronto, I found myself in another system. I had to learn to adjust to a new school and route. The city was much busier than the one we left. Being the new kid in any group can be tricky, but it can be incredibly daunting in those adolescent and teenage years. I felt like a guppy thrown into a shark tank. It didn't help either that I'd grown up in a small town, and Toronto was much louder and rowdier, which made adjusting all the more difficult. Besides, many of the kids at my high school had known each other for years, so I stuck out like a sore thumb. Luckily, it didn't take long for me to start fitting in.

The pool hall was a popular pastime at my high school, so I honed my craft and began to impress the other students by "running the table." Soon enough, I found myself hanging out with some of the more popular kids in school, which did wonders for my self-esteem and confidence. Besides my talent for pool, I had two jobs and didn't mind throwing whatever petty cash I earned around to impress my friends.

Since I had a car, I had an automatic invite to any after-school event, if only for the ride. Suffice it to say I had all the ingredients to fit in when I got out of my head. While I knew some friends only hung out with me so they could hitch a ride, I didn't mind. If anything, I was delighted with the trade-off, feeling it was much better than my early days of walking around the school alone. Things were *great* because I finally felt accepted, so it was easy for me to look the other way when some of my friends started ditching school and getting into trouble. For the most part, I tried to abstain from the worst of it. But there was no denying my priorities had shifted. Playing pool and being cool took precedence over everything else, and I started to coast through school. I settled for doing the bare minimum when I knew I could've performed much better if I had put my mind to it.

Eventually, I could no longer ignore that my friends were becoming a bad influence. When they started to mess around with hard drugs, I couldn't continue to look the other way. The moment I walked away was a real turning point because I realized if I wanted to be "great," I couldn't have negative people holding me back, no matter how harmless their motives might have been.

Negative people can be just as detrimental as negative patterns and behaviors. As you've probably heard a hundred times, "You're the average of the five people you spend the most time with." This saying points out the unavoidable fact that the people around you significantly influence your life.

Have you ever been excited to share a great idea with your friends? You might have been enthusiastic when you talked about the new business you wanted to launch, only to be met with critics and naysayers. You might have even started thinking, "They were right all along; I'm wasting my time, I'm a dreamer, I'm not good enough." Although sometimes critics can be a much-needed voice of reason, the people closest to you should never make you feel less than when correcting you.

We internalize what the closest people to us say and do, so you must have people around you who believe in you and never doubt that you can go the distance. A positive circle of friends will make staying positive easier and getting out of rock bottom easier."

> "I felt lonely for a time, but I knew I wanted to make something of myself, and I could only do that with an active drug scene in the rearview mirror."
>
> Peter Bradford

## The Shift: Victimhood to Empowerment

At rock bottom, it's easy to slip into a victimhood mentality that leaves you powerless and at the mercy of external circumstances. When my marriage ended, it felt like someone had pulled a rug out from under me as I watched my family crumble and my business struggle. It was a scary reality I felt unprepared for, and losing control made me feel helpless.

However, shifting my perspective and reclaiming my agency made me feel empowered. Remembering Jean's words, I was determined to *beebetter*. Knowing that things were spiraling out of control, I had to seek help. I realized I would need more than moping around to help my business get on track or create the close-knit bond I wanted with my daughter.

Instead of going with the flow, I decided to buckle down and be intentional about building a relationship with Emma. Her mother and I may not have seen eye to eye on everything, but I wasn't going to let that stop me from being as physically present as possible.

Luckily, our expansion of Trendy Tactics was starting to pay off, freeing me up to travel more often. With more flexibility, I committed to plan physical meetups with my daughter at least every 45 days. Sometimes, that meant flying to Canada; other times, Emma would make the trip down to visit.

Every day in between, we'd text so I could stay updated on her activities while offering gentle words of motivation when necessary.

I even told clients and business associates to avoid calling me within certain hours when my daughter was with me. It didn't matter what was happening at work. I knew my priorities, as she grew older, we began to have more mature conversations, which allowed me to clarify some of her misconceptions about our relationship and form the foundations of a much more wholesome and stronger bond.

Instead of dwelling on what has happened to you, you can focus on what you can do to improve your current situation. This shift in mindset allowed me to regain control of my life and start making positive changes. Embracing the belief that you can shape your destiny, irrespective of your mistakes, can open you up to new possibilities.

However, if you've spent your life putting your dreams on the back burner for everyone else, it might be harder to change your perspective. You might feel used, unseen, and unappreciated. But the good news is that regardless of your current situation, if you're alive, you can choose your attitude and rise above your lowest points.

Sometimes, changing your perspective is as simple as telling yourself you can. For example, if you suddenly found out you had only six months to live, would you be satisfied with what you've done? If the answer is no, you'd probably make a bucket list of everything you always wanted to do. And you would be much less inclined to put everyone else's needs ahead of yours.

You'd prioritize what you want to do and who you want to be because you'd understand your time was limited. Knowing that life is unpredictable, why don't we live like that daily? Why spend a second longer being "good" when you can be "great"? Ironically, when writing this book, my good friend Lynette was experiencing a rough patch in her mental health. Rather than letting her emotions get the best of her, she chose to circumvent her negative thought patterns by spreading a little joy.

Instead of clamming up and isolating herself, which would inevitably breed toxic thoughts, she embraced motherhood's joys by being present with her children. Whether that was singing made-up songs or acting silly to make them laugh, it was challenging to be in a bad mental space with them.

Lynette also made the extra effort to make other people smile whenever she went out. From servers to checkout assistants, she'd find herself inquiring about their well-being, showing appreciation for their work, and letting them know she was "*buzzing*." Soon enough, these small but intentional steps warmed her heart, putting her on the right path to better days.

That's not to say you should attempt to fake it till you make it when you're clinically depressed. Depression can be debilitating, and it would always be best to seek professional help when experiencing long-term despair and sadness. However, if you dwell in misery and consistently see yourself as a victim, that's what you'll continue to be. But when you're ready to take charge, to shift your perspective, you can empower yourself to *bee* "great."

**Extract Value from Your Situation**

It hurt when I walked away from my high school friends because of their bad habits. I felt lonely for a time, but I knew I wanted to make something of myself, and I could only do that with an active drug scene in the rearview mirror. So, when my parents floated the idea of paying rent while I was home, I jumped at the opportunity to start somewhere else.

For the first time in my life, I instigated a move. My parents no longer dictated where I would go to school or vacation. It was time for me to call the shots. But I knew it was necessary, so I packed my bags, hopped in my car, and bid my parents' farewell.

When I found myself in Ottawa, I'd made the grand leap of moving from my parent's house to my grandmother's house. Still, it was my first experience living alone as my grandmother was on vacation for six weeks, leaving me to explore a new city independently.

Initially, it was daunting, but I had big goals, and the independence was refreshing. Back in Toronto, I'd worked as a waiter at a restaurant called Joe's, and when I moved, I'd asked the manager if it was possible to transfer me to their Ottawa branch.

Over the last year, my boss and I had built a good rapport, so he was happy to help. Within a few days, the paperwork was complete, and I was able to start at Joe's Ottawa branch.

While most of my co-workers found the job repetitive and mundane, I saw it as the opposite. I took it as a challenge, quickly learning to become self-assured when handling customers. Talking to people daily and helping them figure out what they wanted grew my social skills and, more importantly, my self-confidence. I became great at my job and would strive to do it better by remembering customer names and orders.

My memory often blew away regulars, which put a smile on their faces—and knowing that I made their days better if only for a moment made me feel fulfilled, making my job feel like less of a burden.

Eventually, my grandmother returned from vacation and wasn't thrilled with my late hours. At that point, I'd gotten another job stocking shelves at a nearby drugstore. While it meant extra money, I returned at odd hours because I was trying to take on as many shifts as possible.

Although my grandmother understood, she couldn't help but worry. She'd stay up late every night waiting for me to come home, even when I told her not to. When it started to take a toll on her health, we knew something had to change.

*"Peter, I can't do this anymore."* She'd said. *"You know I'm always worried about you being out there."* I understood. Staying up late wasn't healthy for my grandmother, and I had to find an alternative living arrangement. After five months of being only semi-dependent, I moved out for the first time. Besides the stranger who'd become my roommate, I was discovering my strengths and purpose.

Being on my own was tough, but I considered it a training ground for the future. Although I hadn't realized the importance of saying "great" or "buzzing," I was already on the right track. I learned early to cultivate an attitude that allowed me to see the silver lining in any situation. Extracting value from your predicament can give you the resilience to weather the storm and escape rock bottom. One of the biggest lessons I learned while writing this book is how precious life is. While working on this project, I discovered one of my close friends had only a few months to live. After accepting his reality, my friend asked if I would like to help him complete some things on his bucket list.

Though heartbreaking, it gave me a new perspective on how to live in the face of death. Every setback carries valuable lessons and insights to guide you toward a better future and life without regrets.

Even in the darkest moments, there is potential for growth and learning. Extracting value from your rock-bottom experiences can transform adversity into fuel for personal development. Don't blame yourself for where you are. Instead, recognize that it's okay and you can still turn things around.

The skills that I learned at Joe's and while working other odd jobs became invaluable when I went on to work at my first corporate jobs in Nortel and ATC. By then, I understood the importance of diligent service, which helped me build a great rapport with many of the executives at the company.

## Stay Positive in Challenging Times

For many people, traveling can be a high-stress situation, especially during wintertime lousy weather and poor visibility make flight delays and cancellations more frequent, so it's not uncommon to encounter one or two travelers having a terrible day because of these changes.

On one occasion, I had to go on a business trip from Ottawa to California, and we had a stopover at O'Hare International Airport. While I waited for boarding, I overheard another passenger going off at a gate agent because his flight had been postponed.

Judging by his suit and briefcase, the man was traveling on business and wasn't too pleased with the disruption of his schedule as he continued to yell at the agent, demanding to get on the next available flight. "Do you know who I am?" He'd shouted as he tried to intimidate the lady into letting him have his way. Perhaps he thought she secretly had the power to control the weather and was intentionally trying to frustrate him.

To her credit, the gate agent remained calm even when the disgruntled traveler started to swear and curse at her. After several futile minutes of getting nowhere, he stalked away to await the next flight. Embarrassed by the altercation, I approached the gate agent and apologized.

"I'm sorry that guy was terrible to you."

She shrugged as if to say just another day at the office. "You wouldn't believe how many people are like that."

"I can't believe people even blame you. Flight delays aren't your fault." I said sympathetically.

"I know." She replied with another shrug. "But I represent the company, and they get to yell at me."

I was stunned by her maturity and ability to dissociate the criticism of the airline from her person. Realizing being in a bad situation didn't necessarily mean she was at fault or a failure at her job; she could remain calm and diffuse tense situations with volatile travelers.

So even when passengers were yelling and cursing at her due to things that weren't her control, she still felt "great."

I sincerely appreciated her positive attitude and said,

*"I promise I won't yell at you."*

She laughed and politely asked me, "How can I help you?"

"I know the weather is terrible, but could you get me on the next flight? Or is there any chance I could find somewhere to lay my head?"

Ready to help, she tapped at her computer quickly and explained that although she couldn't get me on a flight the same day, she could make accommodation arrangements for me. So, while the disgruntled businessman stewed in an uncomfortable boarding lounge, I enjoyed a free hotel room and food while waiting for my flight.

Although I knew my request was a long shot, the gate agent felt more inclined to help me because, like her, I'd remained positive and pleasant in a challenging situation. By focusing on the blessings that emerge from adversity, we shift our energy towards more positive experiences and can slowly climb out of rock bottom with a smile.

As someone who's worked in sales and has experience scaling small businesses, I can't tell you enough how simply treating people right or joking around over the phone can help you with that extra information. People naturally gravitate towards positive people who treat them with respect, and if you can remember that even when the chips are down, you can come out better in every situation.

**Using Rock Bottom for Self-Reflection**

Rock bottom doesn't define us; it presents an opportunity for growth and transformation. You can rise above your lowest points by identifying negative patterns and people, shifting from a victimhood mentality, and extracting value from your situation. When my life felt like it was crumbling, I chose to remain positive through the storm. And although it was hard, I realized how much I had grown when a close friend of mine went through the same thing at the end of his marriage. Thanks to our shared experience, I could share my story and even crack jokes that brightened the mood.

When I look back, there are certain things I could've done differently when I had the opportunity to spare myself that pain. But I've realized I can only make those decisions retrospectively because I've already lived through it. After all, solving a puzzle is easier when you already know the answer. So when I analyze what I could've done differently, I do so forgivingly, knowing that the Peter I was then wasn't as well-equipped as I am now to handle the same situation.

Like a bee stuck in a house, life can be a puzzle where we're constantly trying to figure the way out of the next jam. If you stick at it long enough, you'll find an opening. We are all human, and we all falter, but it is how we react that defines us, how we stay positive at the very darkest of times that sees us through.

Instead of dwelling on your mistakes and what you don't like or want, you can enjoy a better, healthier, and happier life. However, creating a more positive future can be challenging. Fear, false starts, and doubts are inevitable, so you need the right tools to design your life.

> "Like a bee stuck in a house, life can be a puzzle where we're constantly trying to figure the way out of the next jam."
>
> Peter Bradford

## Chapter 3

## Fear, False Starts, and Doubts

After my enlightening chat with Jean, the VP who'd utterly changed my perspective on how words shape us, I was on cloud 9. Sure, there'd been some back and forth, as I wasn't convinced initially. But I'd witnessed firsthand that replying with "I'm great" instead of "I'm good" was beginning to transform my life. It was barely perceptible initially, and old habits stuck to me like glue for a couple of months. However, through self-will and consistent practice, I began to reflect more on my life, build enthusiasm for my job, and stand out from the crowd. At this point, I decided it was time for a career shift. After 5 years in IT, I wanted to try something new, and since I'd picked an interest in sales and marketing, it was the obvious choice. While I knew it would be no walk in the park, I was young, full of energy and fresh ideas. So, when an opening for a sales support role opened at ATC, I took the plunge.

In the beginning, it seemed like a natural fit. I'd always had a knack for talking with people and felt unstoppable with my newfound "great" attitude. That is until I hit one of my first significant roadblocks.

Early in my career, our senior sales officer entrusted me to present at one of our quarterly corporate meetings. It felt like an obvious choice. After all, I'd been part of the team working on the ingenious sales tool we planned to share. For months, I worked tirelessly on perfecting it.

I knew the solution in and out and was confident it was a brilliant strategy that could change how we did things. Despite my faith in our innovative solution, my confidence in myself faltered.

Sure, I was great at making conversation. But to get on stage in front of 2000 sales guys who knew their stuff, most of whom had been in the industry longer than me, was terrifying. What if I forgot what I was supposed to say? What if I stuttered or made a stupid slip-up? My heart sped up at the thought, my palms felt sweaty, and my stomach relocated to my throat as I contemplated imminent disaster.

Regardless of what stage you are in life right now, you've undoubtedly felt the paralyzing effects of fear, the uncertainty of self-doubt, and the dilemma of false starts. While these seemingly negative emotions can help in dangerous situations, we often react the same way when there's an unprecedented opportunity for progress.

For example, many students consider taking an exam scary because of the possibility of failure. However, taking a test could lead to a higher GPA. If you're already working, it could mean a promotion or the start of a new career. Throughout history, the icy grip of fear, the frustration of false starts, and the relentless onslaught of doubts have gripped countless individuals. Yet, the most outstanding of us aren't those who experience no hesitation; it is those who manage to rise above these negative emotions, even using them to our advantage, to attain extraordinary achievements.

The truth is you cannot outrun the feelings of fear, false starts, and doubts. At some point in our lives, we all experience these emotions, and the most distinctive instance for me was the fear of public speaking. Considering my experience with talking to crowds was limited, distrust in my abilities felt instinctive. These feelings are nothing to be ashamed of, especially since we can work towards overcoming them.

With heightened self-reflection, I realized these emotions were a sign of growth. Evidence that I wasn't in my comfort zone hiding behind computers anymore. I was challenging myself to be "great," to *BeeBetter*.

These pages will confront the paralyzing grip of potential failure and how it holds us back. By embracing the power of change and shifting our perspective from "good" to "great," we can learn to harness the limitations of fear, false starts, and doubt, transforming them into a window for growth and achievement.

## Understanding Fear

My stomach plummeted when the senior sales officer informed me I would face an entire audience of sales gurus. I spent several hours reviewing my notes the night before, worried I'd forget something important. Despite memorizing my notes off-hand, I was still quite nervous as the dreaded day finally arrived. I could barely concentrate during the corporate meeting while waiting for my turn on stage. My mind continued to play every worst-case scenario.

I conjured images of everyone laughing at me as I stuttered or my colleagues shaking their heads, disappointed because my presentation wasn't good enough. As I pictured such scenes, my entire body vibrated with fear.

I'd read online that breaking the ice with a joke would improve things. But I still had my doubts. What if nobody thought the joke was funny, and they didn't laugh? Had I made a mistake by leaving IT and jumping to sales? All these questions swirled in my head until the floor was finally mine. With my stomach in my throat and heavy legs, I went backstage to await my cue and ascended the stairs. I anxiously gripped the mic, whispered to myself, "You're going to be great," and spoke.

I delivered the joke I'd rehearsed and waited. It must've been a few milliseconds, but it felt like an eternity, then a smile—a chuckle. Two chuckles. And the entire audience broke into a small fit of laughs. With the ice cracked and reassured by my preparedness, I gave an excellent sales pitch. In retrospect, that speech was a turning point in my life. I realized that during my pitch, I was not afraid.

I'd taken the necessary precautions to succeed at this task and gave it my all. That event boosted my confidence and helped me unlock another superb skill: public speaking. I'd climbed the stage as a nervous rookie, and descended as a confident salesman, ready to take on a larger audience. All the worst-case scenarios I'd imagined seemed like ludicrous delusions, and it felt like all my fear was unnecessary. I realized then that fear only exists in anticipation.

Think about it. When were you last afraid, and how did you feel after finally getting on with it? Your hesitation is often at its peak just before you climb the stage, air your opinions, or say yes to a new opportunity. But as soon as you say, "Yes, I will face my fears - I'm going to be great," - it has no power over you. It reminded me of George Addair's quote, "Everything you've ever wanted is on the other side of fear."

Don't get me wrong; fear is a primal emotion deeply ingrained in our biology and psychology to help us survive as a species. Fear was helpful to our ancestors when they encountered a lion in the wild. The potentially threatening situation would trigger several physiological responses, including increased heart rate, heightened senses, and the release of stress hormones like adrenaline. These bodily changes would enable them to react swiftly and fight off the threat or flee from it.

However, in the modern world, you're less likely to encounter a wild animal that isn't in a cage. Instead, our worst nightmares come from our distaste for failure, rejection, criticism, or the unknown, which can often hinder our progress and personal growth.

Like we absentmindedly do when we say, "I'm fine," it creates a psychological barrier that keeps us within our comfort zones, discouraging us from taking risks or pursuing our dreams. When we allow fear to control our actions, we remain stagnant. We recoil into our comfort zone, which can be dangerous because it means missing out on opportunities for self-improvement and fulfillment. So, since fear is inevitable, how do we learn to leverage it so it doesn't stop us from being "great."

## Appropriate and Disproportionate Fear

The essence of this chapter is not to demonize fear. On the contrary, it is to help you harness disproportionate fear. Which begs the question, what is the difference between appropriate and disproportionate fear? Appropriate fears are based on genuine threats to our well-being and safety. For instance, feeling fear when faced with a physical danger like a charging animal or street burglar is an appropriate response that can help us protect ourselves. On the other hand, disproportionate fears are often exaggerated compared to the actual threat or rooted in unfounded beliefs.

Our imagination, past experiences, or societal conditioning are more likely to drive these fears. Of course, that's not to say these worries are illegitimate. Starting a new career, moving to a new city, or asking for help can be rightfully scary.

But when these fears become so overwhelming, they disrupt our daily lives and hinder us from attaining our goals, they become disproportionate. My fear of public speaking gained momentum from my hyperactive imagination about what could go wrong, my lack of experience, and a slight feeling of intimidation as I addressed a crowd of my peers.

Was it unusual to feel anxious? Not at all. But in hindsight, I understand now that it was a disproportionate fear because I let it rob me of my peace of mind. I allowed it to cloud my resolution to be "great." Looking inward, you might realize you have a similar fear of trying something new, making mistakes, or having confrontational conversations.

Recognizing the difference between appropriate and disproportionate fear empowers us to confront and overcome the former. While reasonable fears could be a matter of life and death, disproportionate fears tell us something important is at stake, such as our sense of belonging, self-esteem, status, or fulfillment.

My confidence as a salesman and standing with my colleagues hinged on my presentation. But even if my pitch wasn't up to par, I would've had other opportunities to redeem myself or learn a valuable lesson. Once you realize that 99% of what you fear will not kill you, combining this knowledge with a "great" attitude can help you embrace calculated risks. With a determination to *BeeBetter*, you can make intentional choices that have you running after your goals instead of shying away from opportunities.

# Impact of Fear on Decision-Making

Fear significantly influences our decision-making processes. When fear dominates our thoughts and emotions, we prioritize short-term comfort and safety over long-term growth and fulfillment.

For example, you might need to work on getting a new job or starting a completely different career if you hate your job. Or your fear of being single could prevent you from having difficult conversations with your partner or walking out on a relationship you know isn't healthy.

Because of their uncertainty, these disproportionate fears prevent us from pursuing new opportunities, projects, or relationships. However, according to psychologists at Cornell University, 85% of what people worry about never happens. With that statistic in mind, it's safe to say that your worst-case scenarios are unlikely to happen. When I got on the stage with trembling fingers during my presentation, I played out all the terrible things that could happen. What if no one laughs at my jokes? What if I stink? What if my boss realizes he made a huge mistake by trusting me? In the end, my speech was a lot better than I expected.

If you remember the past, I'm sure you'll remember some situations where things turned out much better than anticipated. Overcoming fear involves recognizing that growth often occurs outside of our comfort zones, and you must be willing to remind yourself that things won't only be good; they'll be great.

## Recognizing False Starts

Refers to our attempts towards a goal or transformation that ultimately leads to limited or no progress. Think about the last time you tried to pick up a new habit or explore a business idea. You might have started with a lot of well-intentioned enthusiasm that fizzled out when you didn't get the expected results.

Quitting a job, you hate in pursuit of a freelance career or launching your startup can be scary, especially when things aren't going according to plan.

This phase is significant because it can be discouraging when you don't hit the ground running. However, when you let your false starts demotivate you, you lose momentum, derailing your journey toward greatness. As I highlighted in the previous chapter, it's crucial to stay positive in challenging times and see your setbacks as an opportunity. A great example of a famous person who experienced a false start is Walt Disney, the visionary behind the Walt Disney Company and beloved characters like Mickey Mouse. In the early days of his career, Walt Disney faced a series of failures and setbacks.

One notable instance was when he started his first animation company, Laugh-O-Gram Studios, in Kansas City, Missouri. Disney envisioned creating a series of modernized fairy tales, but the venture struggled financially and eventually went bankrupt. Undeterred by this setback, Disney packed his bags and moved to Hollywood, California, in 1923 with his brother Roy Disney.

They founded the Disney Brothers Studio, which later evolved into the Walt Disney Studio. However, even after relocating, Disney faced more challenges. His first few attempts at creating animated films, such as "Alice's Wonderland" and "Oswald the Lucky Rabbit," faced difficulty finding distribution deals and were met with limited success.

Luckily, Disney's turning point came in 1928 when he introduced a new character, Mickey Mouse, in the animated short film "Steamboat Willie." This iconic creation marked the birth of the Disney empire and propelled Walt Disney to worldwide recognition.

Through resilience and determination, Walt Disney overcame financial hardships, business failures, and creative obstacles. He never gave up on his dreams. His ability to adapt, innovate, and create enduring characters and stories ultimately led to the immense success of the Walt Disney Company, which has become synonymous with entertainment and magic.

Whatever setbacks you face right now, remember that they are temporary. You'll succeed with a vision for greatness and an attitude to match.

> "Not every false start is an inevitable setback you must overcome. Some false starts are avoidable and are products of unpreparedness."
>
> Peter Bradford

# Reasons Behind False Starts

## Lack of Clarity

Not every false start is an inevitable setback you must overcome. Some false starts are avoidable and are products of unpreparedness. For example, I decided to try something else when I discovered the corporate world wasn't for me. Falling back on my interests, I delved into marketing and decided to set up a venture assisting small businesses in scaling up their visibility. When my partners and I wanted to expand, our company hit a lull, and it felt like we were doing too much too fast. Despite the challenges, we clearly understood our goals and knew the steps we were taking were necessary. Did we have to reevaluate some of our plans? Certainly. But clarity on when, how, and what to do next made it easier to prepare and take the proper steps.

## Feeling Overwhelmed

False starts can manifest as feeling overwhelmed by the enormity of the task ahead. Sometimes, when we have a lot to do, instead of getting to it, we can wind up in a state of analysis paralysis or inaction.

Have you ever found yourself contemplating a significant change? You should get around to hitting the gym like you said you would for ages. But the thought of lifting weights and running on a treadmill terrifies you. You wonder how long it will take to achieve your health goals when you get winded just from climbing the stairs. Not to mention, you must check the reviews of different gyms and alter your current schedule. With so many things to do, you leave it on your to-do list and never get around to it despite consistently contemplating it. What's overwhelming you is an essential assignment with a pending deadline. So, you tell yourself, I must get it right. It must be perfect, and you delay until you can no longer procrastinate.

But inaction doesn't always mean doing nothing. Sometimes, we can even deceive ourselves into thinking we're making progress when we're not. You could get stuck in the planning phase of your assignment, doing the research and saving resources without writing anything. Or, applying this to our earlier example, if you want to go to the gym, you can buy new workout shoes or subscribe to a membership plan without going to the gym.

However, when you ask yourself, "What will it take to make today great?" "How can I feel buzzing?" It inspires you to act and spurs you to rise above these false starts, motivating you to write, hit the gym, or act in other ways.

**Shifting Priorities**

False starts can crop up when we continuously shift focus. People who change their goals consistently are more likely to encounter this problem because it prevents them from making sustained progress in any direction. Instead of failing to start, the situation becomes remaining consistent on a set path.

For example, you might not struggle to hit the gym, but you find yourself starting multiple fitness programs and abandoning them halfway through to pursue the latest trend. Changing your routine is fine if something isn't working for you. But constantly jumping on the newest fad will leave you feeling burnt out.

Although I started my career in IT and moved on to sales before finally settling in marketing and business development, I stuck to each career path for years. I gave myself time to discover my strengths and passions before moving on to the next thing. When Laugh-O-Gram studios failed, Walt Disney didn't pack up shop and sell ice cream. He stuck to his passions, created a new company, and established characters that would be recognizable for decades to come. Being at rock bottom doesn't necessarily mean jumping ship. You need to analyze your situation and create a plan that allows you to remain consistent in whatever you're doing to achieve great results.

## Consequences of Allowing False Starts to Persist

**Self-Doubt**

Persistent false starts can lead to frustration, self-doubt, and a lack of confidence in our ability to make meaningful changes. Back to our example of going to the gym, false starts stemming from a lack of consistency or inaction can create frustration when we fail to see progress.

This lack of progress can trigger internal negative self-talk and blame. You might think, "Maybe I'm not working hard enough," or "Maybe I'm just not good enough." It could also lead to us comparing ourselves unfavorably to others, reinforcing feelings of inadequacy, self-doubt, and fear.

**Self-Sabotage**

Beyond making us question our abilities, false starts can be a recipe for self-sabotage. Have you ever found yourself putting in a lackluster performance at work or in an application because the thought of being rejected terrified you? It might sound odd, but sometimes, we work against ourselves to give us more control when things don't go as planned. After all, when we perform poorly, our results match our efforts. False starts can be driven by a fear of failure, causing us to hold back or sabotage our efforts before even giving ourselves a chance to succeed. Self-doubt and self-sabotage are intertwined and can drain our motivation, enthusiasm, and self-esteem.

Unfortunately, when we act against ourselves, creating results that confirm our inner self-doubt, it only demoralizes us. But by acknowledging the consequences of allowing false starts to persist, we can take proactive steps to overcome them. Recognizing the reasons behind our false starts is crucial for personal growth because it will enable us to identify patterns and behaviors that hinder our progress. Through self-reflection, goal setting, and a willingness to push through challenges, we can transform false starts into meaningful and sustained progress from "good" to "great".

## Jumping Over Doubts

Doubts are the thoughts and feelings of uncertainties we experience when we question our abilities, worthiness, or likelihood of success. Doubts appear harmless, but when we let them restrict our actions, they can significantly erode our self-confidence and hinder our transformation.

Doubt can also lead to a fear of success, where we sabotage ourselves due to the fear of handling the responsibilities and expectations of achieving our goals. This phenomenon can manifest as Imposter syndrome, which is incredibly common. According to Workplace Insights, 3 in 5 workers experience imposter syndrome, and Harvard Business Review reports that at least 70% of us will experience it at some point.

When I first had my daughter, I was ecstatic. Emma was a fantastic baby, and the first three days at the hospital were bliss. After every meal, she would go to bed and sleep until the next feeding time. It felt like I'd had hacked parenting on day one.

Unfortunately, that mindset didn't last long. It was havoc when my ex-wife and I eventually took our newborn daughter home on day four. She cried non-stop for five hours on the first night, refused to be soothed, and seemed to increase her pitch within 5 feet of her crib. I felt helpless. What if I can't figure out a way to make her stop crying? Maybe I was in over my head? What if I wasn't cut out to be a parent after all? Eventually, we figured out that the change in environment kept Emma up and cranky.

The hospital had been bright, noisy, and full of chaos, and although that might not have been what I considered prime sleeping conditions, it was what our newborn had grown accustomed to. When we finally switched on the lights, she fell asleep instantly.

Like fear, my self-doubt was disproportionate. I'd barely been a parent for a week and was setting unrealistic expectations of getting everything right. After getting out of my head and figuring out the problem, I felt secure in my abilities and that I would always be enough.

### Recognizing Self-doubt

Self-doubt often stems from past experiences, influences, comparisons to others, or fear of failure. Fear and self-doubt are closely intertwined, so understanding the connection between the two is essential for addressing and overcoming doubts.

### Be More Mindful

Take time to identify and reflect on the specific doubts that hold you back. Developing mindfulness can help you catch negative thought patterns and why they exist. You might make excuses or find distractions when addressing an issue with your partner or asking for a raise at work. You might also notice that some of your doubt comes from a place of disproportionate fear. Remember, you don't necessarily need to engage with these thoughts; observing them alone by simply being present can help you.

## Embrace Self-Compassion

Often, we're too hard on ourselves, expecting perfection we don't ask of others. So, when we encounter challenges, it can be difficult to remember self-compassion when doubt creeps into the picture. Ask yourself why you doubt your abilities and how past experiences may influence your self-perception. As a young father, I was apprehensive because I'd never undertaken anything quite like parenting.

Plus, working in IT support and sales in a big corporate firm didn't exactly give me transferable skills when putting an infant to sleep. But I had to learn to cut myself some slack. Sure, I was learning on my feet like I'd done all those years ago when I first ventured into computers, but I was determined to be a great parent. As Emma continued to grow, so did I, and even though it wasn't perfect, it didn't have to be.

> "Ask yourself why you doubt your abilities and how past experiences may influence your self-perception."
>
> Peter Bradford

## Piercing Through Doubt

**Embrace Failure as Learning**

Recognize that failure is a natural part of growth. Your first day at the gym might be a struggle. You might be pumped and ready to run on the treadmill for 15 minutes but quickly realize you're too out of shape. Imagine how disappointing it would be to know you can barely get up to 3 minutes.

When many of us fall short during exercise or in other areas, we often doubt our self-worth. Instead of viewing failure as confirmation of your limitations, you can view it as an opportunity to assess your current cardio status.

With a better understanding of what your body can do, you can start to set more realistic expectations. After a month or two of going to the gym consistently, you can set a goal to run for 15 minutes at a stretch. And if you want to stick to your plan, you can break it down.

Breaking your goals into smaller, manageable steps makes it easier to build momentum and confidence. Remember that perfection doesn't exist, so be willing to cut yourself some slack on the days you're too busy to go or feel winded early.

Understand that, like adopting the habit of saying, "I'm great," progress takes time.

## Celebrate Your Successes

Acknowledge and celebrate your achievements, no matter how small. Instead of merely breathing a sigh of relief after completing my sales pitch without a hitch, I mentally applauded myself. I'd been great, excellent even. And that spurred me to see myself as someone capable of public speaking. What had once been a major flaw was an untapped asset.

You need to recognize your progress, no matter how small. Reinforcing a positive self-image will help you go further than self-doubt ever will. Whatever you've achieved could also be a powerful reminder of your capabilities during moments of doubt—dreading an exam? Remember that you've spent countless hours preparing. Anxious about a new project? Think about how well the last one went or what you learned. Celebrating your seemingly minor achievements thus far can help you ward off self-doubt.

## Surround Yourself with Positivity

Seek out supportive and uplifting influence. Surrounding yourself with people who believe in you and encourage your growth waters down your negative self-talk. Whenever I would reply with "I'm great," it would automatically inspire me to do better. It would also motivate the people around me to be better listeners, as they would often be intrigued by my unusually positive response. And when people were more inclined to listen, it made my job as a salesperson much easier.

Awareness of how people make you feel can help you shed the overbearing voices in your head. On the other hand, people who overstep their boundaries and belittle you can trigger negative self-talk cycles that consistently make you question your worth and abilities.

In high school, I had to distance myself from the people I called friends when I was no longer comfortable with their behavior and values. With some awareness, you can identify such people in your life. If you do, you don't need to treat them awfully. There's no reason to be as dramatic as Alan Sugar saying, "You're fired!" in the BBC reality show, The Apprentice. But you do have to decide enough is enough and strategically pull away from these negative influences and continually grow your circle of people who positively reinforce the great self you're becoming.

**Take Action Despite Doubts**

Finally, it's crucial to realize that self-doubt can spur from disproportionate fear and false starts, and the key to overcoming these obstacles lies in acting. If you want to breed confidence in yourself, step out of your comfort zone and act towards your goals. Starting with small steps will gradually push your boundaries and build your self-esteem and worth.

Overcoming doubts requires a combination of self-reflection, mindset shifts, and practical action. When you understand the origins of self-doubt, it makes it easier to challenge those negative thoughts.

And when self-doubt gives way to confidence, it diminishes your mental restraints and can pave the way for personal transformation. Remember, self-belief is the key to unlocking your true potential and embracing the journey from "good" to "great."

**scan me.**
Get your free workbook to help jumpstart your journey.
#word?

**thank you.**
You can also visit www.beebettermovement.com and download the free workbook from there.

## Embracing Fear, False Starts, and Doubts

Whenever I have a new challenge, I remember my first sales pitch. The nerves, the fear, and the doubt all washed away when I spoke about what I was passionate about with confidence. Knowing that made me keenly aware that if I could dig deep and overcome that obstacle, I could do the same for any setback.

In this chapter, we have delved into fear, false starts, and doubts, recognizing their influence in our lives and their potential to hinder our journey from "good" to "great." We have come to understand that these obstacles are not insurmountable barriers but opportunities for growth and transformation.

Fear, that ever-present companion, has the power to paralyze us, to keep us confined within the boundaries of our comfort zones. But it is not a signal that should be ignored; instead, disproportionate fear is a guide, pointing us toward the areas of our lives that require our attention and courage. The moment before you get on a rollercoaster is always the scariest. But when you finally get on, there's no more room to be scared, you only feel the thrill and of course, nauseousness.

In life, starting a new career, having difficult conversations, and public speaking are necessary rides that you must get on to achieve greatness. When you embrace the courage to work through the fear and step into the unknown, you open yourself to new possibilities and unforeseen accomplishments.

False starts and setbacks are a natural part of any journey toward greatness. They test our resilience, challenge our determination, and force us to confront our weaknesses. Instead of viewing them as failures, you should see them as valuable lessons and stepping stones to success.

With clarity, action, and a focused priority, you can get closer to finding the right direction. Doubts, those nagging voices questioning our abilities and potential, can erode our self-belief.

However, we recognize that doubt is not a sign of weakness but rather an opportunity for self-reflection and growth. By acknowledging our doubts and investigating their origins, we can confront them head-on and replace them with a stronger sense of self-belief.

In conclusion, fear, false starts, and doubts are not roadblocks to greatness; they are integral to your transformative journey. By embracing fear, learning from false starts, and confronting doubts, we gain resilience and the confidence needed to propel ourselves beyond the realm of the ordinary.

Together, let us embrace discomfort, push beyond our limits, and dare to embark on a life of greatness by transforming the ordinary into the extraordinary.

## Chapter 4

## **Changing Inside, Design Your Own Life**

In the summer of 2008, DreamWorks released the start of one of their most successful franchises, Kung Fu Panda. Seeing a fluffy panda perform martial arts wasn't exactly on my bucket list for the holidays, but Emma was eager to see it, and it allowed us to bond. Our family-friendly cinema date quickly became a moment of introspection, as the protagonist, Po, went from a clumsy student to a kung fu master. It was complete with a training sequence where the main character realizes all he's ever needed to be great is already inside him.

If you've ever watched an action or adventure movie with an underdog, you've most likely seen the "internal motivation turns to exterior power" motif. That moment where our hero is on a losing streak, possibly even down, and the villain is about to clinch victory.

The bad guy might even take the opportunity to boast and bask in the hero's despair. However, when all hope seems lost, at the last minute, the protagonist recalls some of their best moments, advice from a mentor, or the sacrifices of their loved ones and rises again.

The music amps as they stand to their feet, experiencing what they call a heroic second wind in cinema. Suddenly, after experiencing a drastic mental shift, our hero has the upper hand despite enduring severe injuries and loss.

And in a remarkable show of strength that leaves the villain enraged, confused, or contrite, the protagonist saves the day. It's a theme we've all seen and loved; it might even be in your favorite movie or TV show. The moment where the hero's internal realization births immense power and enables them to turn the tables is a popular trope many people can relate to. But this trope doesn't exist in fantasy alone.

It can also translate to the real world. Yours might get a sudden burst of energy to finish a paper due the next day or a stellar display of strength, speed, and flexibility when someone you love is in trouble. And while these sudden bursts of talent and power are momentary, it shows a trend we can all use to our advantage.

Change starts inwardly, whether it's a spark or a long-term commitment to transform your life for the better. Everything we've covered in this book so far points to the power of shifting your perspective first before taking action to elevate your life from good to great.

From realizing the importance of choosing your words carefully to picking yourself up from rock bottom and overcoming your fears, it all requires the right internal mindset. So, in this chapter, we'll delve deeper into personal growth, focusing on how changing on the inside can help you design a great life.

## Understanding the Power of Internal Change

If you're reading this book, I know at least one thing about you: you're looking for change in your life. You're looking to *BeeBetter*. There are many reasons people read self-help books: to get better at making money, to learn how to make friends, to find long-forgotten secrets to being happy, and much more. But regardless of what sub-genre of self-help book you like, the burden of putting it to use remains on the reader.

While preparing for this project we did a lot of research about how people respond to books and even until now, I still find it fascinating that two people could have different outcomes after reading the same book.

Jack might view it as a collection of wise words with an exciting concept, while it could be a life-changing experience for Kelly, a turning point in her life to make better choices and take more positive actions.

Jack returns to his everyday life, unchanged by what he read except for a couple of cool quotes that he shared on social media, while Kelly enjoys a more fulfilling life after finding the answers to some of her problems. So, while the source material remains the same, these two readers would have significantly different results because, unlike Jack, something clicked on the inside for Kelly.

In essence, the power of internal change can be the difference between returning to your everyday life after completing this book or going on to change your world.

When you work on improving your thoughts, feelings, and behaviors from within, you can positively shape your life. Likewise, when you work on going from "good" to "great," your mindset shift makes it possible to *BeeBetter*.

## The Power of Visualization

Visualization is a powerful tool used by athletes, artists, and successful people from all walks of life. Consistently visualizing your objectives allows you to create a mental map that guides your actions. When I started asking myself the big question, "What will it take to be great?" I became more mindful about where my life was heading. Whenever I used my buzzword, I asked myself if my life was true to my reply.

And I felt like it wasn't. I would mentally conjure an image of what would've been. Envisioning your ideal life gives you a clear direction and a sense of purpose. So, I was always looking to achieve a higher degree of greatness, which would help me align my choices with my desired outcome. As the famous saying goes, "If you think you can do it, you can."

So, visualize your goals, dreams, and aspirations as they are happening now. I believe in the power of visualization so much that I often use it when working with my clients. I always start by asking my clients their goals, as that shapes my strategies to help them move forward.

Envisioning the future, you desire helps your subconscious mind work diligently to bridge the gap between your current reality and your ideal future. It also makes it easier to stay on track when designing a great life.

## The Power of Affirmation

An affirmation is a positive statement that challenges and overcomes self-sabotaging and negative thoughts. They serve as a daily reminder of your capabilities and worth. For instance, if you're striving for a career change, you might affirm, "I am skilled and confident, and I am worthy of a fulfilling career." Repeating your affirmation reinforces your belief in yourself and counters self-doubt. Over time, you'll find that your affirmations become your inner cheering squad, boosting your confidence and motivation.

Visualization and affirmations often go hand in hand. While the former focuses on envisioning the ideal life, the latter takes it further by dealing with the present. Many famous people believe in the power of affirmations, including Oprah Winfrey. Born into poverty in rural Mississippi, life wasn't easy. However, the favorite American talk show host has shared several times that she would only be where she is with a positive mindset. Although she had a difficult childhood, she knew she was destined for greatness and exhibited exceptional charisma at a young age.

Knowing she wanted better than what she was born into, she sprang into action and got a job as a radio host, eventually setting the foundation of her career as one of America's most influential talk show hosts. Despite the setbacks she'd been dealt in life, she became one of the most prestigious media figures, inspiring millions worldwide through her shows, philanthropy, and advocacy efforts. Your Affirmation asserts your role as the designer of your life and reinforces your desired beliefs or behavior, like sticking to a buzzword.

Besides cultivating a positive mindset, affirmations can boost confidence, reduce stress, and improve emotional well-being. I've always been a fan of visualization. It's a key component of my success and increases the likelihood of manifesting my goals. Here's a quick step-by-step guide that works for me in crafting affirmations.

**Visualize Your Goal:**

Affirmations are complete with a focus on the desired outcome. Whenever I have work to do, I imagine what I want to achieve, which is often in line with my client's desires. Write it down or create a vision board that makes it more tangible. It could be related to personal growth, self-confidence, health, relationships, or other aspects of your life.

**Choose Positive Language:**

I focus my affirmations on what I want to achieve rather than what I'm avoiding. The words we use to communicate with ourselves, and others profoundly impact our thoughts, feelings, and behaviors. Phrases like "I don't want to suck at work" or "I'll try to be good at my job" can create a negative mindset and limit your potential. By saying, "I will do great in my career," we express determination and commitment. This language change can help us achieve our goals and overcome obstacles.

**Make it Personal:**

Affirmations should be personal as they focus on specific goals. "I'll become a world-renowned talk show host" clearly won't work for you if that's not your dream.

Be clear about the desired outcome you want to manifest and say it in the first person with "I" or "I am" to claim ownership of the affirmation.

**Use Empowering Words:**

We often underestimate a word's power to inspire, motivate, or even hold us back. The entire theme of this book is about how selecting words that evoke strong positive emotions can transform your life and open you up to new possibilities. Use words like "great," "confident," "abundant," or any other word that resonates with your goal.

Including your buzzword in your affirmations can also help the habit of using it stick. Remember that consistency and repetition are essential when using affirmations. Integrating them into your daily routine can positively influence your mindset and actions as you work towards designing the ideal life.

> "We often underestimate a word's power to inspire, motivate, or even hold us back."
>
> Peter Bradford

## Unleashing Your Potential

Self-reflection is like a mirror for your soul. It's the practice of looking inward to examine your thoughts, feelings, and experiences. By understanding your past and present, you can clarify your aspirations. If you want to design a life you love, you must unleash your potential, and to do that, you need to understand the blueprint of your inner self.

When I discovered the benefits of using more positive words to describe myself, I focused on self-reflection. I'd always been good, but it'd only occurred to me then to be great. So, when I started replying to conversations with, "I'm great," it boosted my confidence.

My newfound buzzword was most authentic when actively engaging other people and not only internalizing it. When I reflect on the jobs I've had, I was always at my best when I was talking to others. Suddenly empowered with greatness, I recognized it as a strength. With time, the answer to the question, "What will it take to make today great?" became apparent.

It was talking to people, sharing their burdens, and helping them gain clarity. Besides, when I envisioned my life at 18, my goals were to own a business that allowed me to work from anywhere and retire at 45. Knowing what I could do and what I wanted led me to become intentional about my job. It was no longer only about keeping the lights on; it was about moving toward my dreams.

My internal self-reflection would lead me to pursue sales and, eventually, a marketing career. By gaining clarity about who I was and still am, I made intentional steps to lay the foundation of my career.

If you want to unleash your potential and make a hero's comeback, reflect on your deepest desires and aspirations. Take the time to explore your values, passions, strengths, and weaknesses. Ask yourself what truly matters to you. What makes you come alive? And when do you feel the most authentic when you reply with great, excellent, superb, or whatever your buzzword is? Understanding your inner architecture allows you to align your actions and choices with your authentic self.

It enables you to make decisions that align with your values, leading to a more fulfilling and purpose-driven life. It involves exploring your interests, pushing your boundaries, and uncovering hidden aspects of yourself. Engage in activities that pique your curiosity and passion. Try new experiences, step out of your comfort zone, and learn from successes and failures.

## Shifting Your Mindset

Since I discovered that it only takes one word to *bee*better, I've been enthusiastic about sharing the secret. I've always been a giver, so whenever I have the opportunity, I tell my friends, family, and colleagues how swapping "good" for "great" has been life changing.

I've found that, often, the people I tell fall into one of two groups: those with a closed mindset and those with an open mindset. People with a closed mindset often disregard my advice, instead sticking with automatic replies that do little to help them grow.

On the other hand, people with an open mindset are more eager to apply the same principle to their lives or at least give it a shot. Nine out of ten times, the people with an open mindset come back to thank me.

When faced with setbacks, individuals with an open mindset can use their buzzwords to reframe failure as an opportunity for growth and view it as an opportunity for growth rather than failure.

**The Power of an Open Mindset**

Life is dynamic. People with an open mindset are more likely to be flexible, and designing your life requires adaptability. Even with the most realistic outlook, life often throws curveballs that might push your goals further away or make them seem out of reach. In those moments, it's crucial to learn to roll with the new status quo and go back to the drawing board.

However, embracing flexibility does not mean abandoning your vision or goals; instead, it means being open to different paths and approaches. When I turned 20, I decided to buy a house. Financial independence was always one of my primary goals, and I already understood the importance of owning equity.

I pictured coming home after a long day of work to a place I could call mine and the freedom of living on my terms without anyone else interfering. Still, it was a bit of a reach at a young age, and I needed help.

I'd always looked up to my grandmother, and she was the easy choice when discussing money matters. She taught me how to budget and manage money when I was 14, and I still use many of the valuable lessons I learned from her today.

When I approached her about my dream of buying a house, she didn't laugh or turn me away based on my youth. She knew my aspirations were bold, and I was willing to work. So, we sat down and created a budget to determine if I could afford the house of my dreams. Of course, I came up short. My dreams of solo living were out of reach at the time if I wanted to stay out of debt. Still, it didn't mean homeownership was entirely out of the question. I knew I needed roommates if I wanted to be a property owner. Sure, I wouldn't have the freedom I craved, but I'd still live under my roof, which sounded great.

My grandmother was happy to loan me the cash for the down payment, and with two jobs, I could easily make the monthly repayments. I still needed roommates to help with other bills, so I planned to rent out all three rooms in my newly bought house.

I convinced my sister and her husband to rent the master, and I had two other friends take one space each. I could cover utilities and save money with tenants in all three rooms. Knowing that I was making extra cash, I was happy to make my living quarters in the basement, which also served as the location for my business.

Although the new living arrangement I found myself in hadn't been what I'd initially dreamt of, it was an opportunity to appreciate the value of being flexible and adaptable. When you use your buzzword, even when things aren't going the way you want, it keeps you open to new opportunities that may arise unexpectedly. Stay committed to your vision and allow room for growth and evolution.

Remaining flexible means adjusting your plans and embracing detours when necessary. Remembering that was instrumental in preventing me from dwelling at rock bottom when my family split. But I accepted the fact distance wouldn't stop me from having a great relationship with my daughter, and even though it took a lot of effort for us to get on track, it was worth it.

In designing your life, you must remain flexible. With an open mindset, you can make your buzzword stick, helping you overcome challenges, pursue your dreams, and live a more fulfilling life.

## How to Effectively Shift Your Mindset

If you have closed mind and barely try out new concepts or listen to reason it can be hard to change on the inside and even harder to use your new buzzword. But with a lot of effort and determination, you can slowly become a little but more open minded and start to gradually shift your mindset.

### Be Aware of Your Current Mindset:

The first step is to consider your thoughts. In our fast-paced world, mindfulness is a crucial practice to observe where your mind is. If you think, "I can't do this" while reading this book or have negative thoughts like "I'm not good enough." That's your starting point.

### Challenge Negative Thoughts:

If you determine that you have a closed mindset, the next step should be challenging these negative thoughts. When you catch yourself closing off, challenge it. Ask yourself, "Is this thought helping me, or is it holding me back?"

### Replace with Positivity:

After you've uprooted those negative thoughts, replace them with positive ones. Instead of "I can't do this," try "I can learn and improve." Using affirmations that channel an open mindset can help you successfully shift in the right direction.

**Practice Gratitude:**

Gratitude is a powerful mindset shifter. There's a whole chapter on it in this book. Focusing on the good stuff in your life makes it easier to adopt your buzzword without feeling like you're pretending. It's more authentic to say, "I'm fantastic," and mean it after thinking about how lucky you are to have your kids or how fantastic your new job is. Remember, Gratitude is a BeeBetter Attitude.

**Change Your Environment:**

Just like plants need a good environment, you need positive people and influences around you. Spend time with those who lift and inspire you; their positivity can rub off on you, making you more receptive. Shifting your mindset takes time and effort, but the more open you are to adopting a "great" mindset, the easier it becomes.

## Designing Your Life

Designing your life is an empowering move that requires changing on the inside first. Like any hero, beating the bad guy and carving a path toward victory requires an internal mindset shift. A change on the inside that empowers you to take charge of your life and become the instigator of your destiny.

Recognizing the power of visualization and affirmations can help you consistently seek personal growth. Staying upbeat has been instrumental in helping me through rock bottom and battle the fears and doubts that sprung up when I started to have a swift career.

Affirmations may not bring about immediate changes, but they can keep you confident as you embrace an internal transformative journey. In this chapter, we've explored the tools and practices that can guide your transformation.

Embrace them as you embark on the journey of designing your own life. You are the artist, the architect, and the author of your destiny.

With dedication, patience, and unwavering belief in yourself, you can craft a life that reflects your deepest desires and aspirations, one brushstroke at a time.

**scan me.**
Get your free workbook to help jumpstart your journey.
#word?

**thank you.**
You can also visit www.beebettermovement.com and download the free workbook from there.

## Chapter 5

### Changing The Outside, Fake It Till You Make It

Actors are phenomenal; whether it's a play or a full-length movie, they pull us into an alternate reality as they embody their characters. Adorned in elaborate outfits and makeup, they make us believe they are someone completely different from who they are. A reincarnation of a character from a book or history comes alive. So what if I told you that the mere act of changing yourself, of momentarily "faking it," offers a significant secret to your success and personal development?

"Faking it" is rarely about external validation. It isn't about pretending to be someone you're not; it's about stepping outside your comfort zone and embodying the person you aspire to become. And that taps into the fundamental core of this book when you say, "I'm great, excellent, or buzzing."

If I'm to be completely honest, I did falter. At rock bottom, nothing about my life felt excellent, and trying to be positive even hurt. When I told people I was great, close friends and family called me out. They told me I wasn't being genuine; how could I be great when so many bad things were happening?

You may be struggling with something, experiencing a downturn in your business, or recently losing a loved one. But like my former boss, Jean, said: You are always great as a person, even when bad things happen.

It might be hard to remain positive in your current situation, but with confidence and determination to change how you react to whatever life throws at you, you can begin the journey to switch on the outside.

After exploring the concepts of overcoming fear, self-doubt, and internal change, it's only natural to discuss how the journey from "good" to "great" requires outward change. As I highlighted in the first chapter of this book, the shift from replying with "fine" to responding with a more enthusiastic buzzword is something you can start immediately.

You may have tried to work "great" into your daily vocabulary already. However, the most common feedback I get from friends and family is that it initially feels inauthentic.

You might find it feels like you're pretending or even lying. And that's why "Faking It Till You Make It" is a powerful tool for transformation in the pursuit of personal growth.

The principal behind these five words is based on the idea that by imitating the behaviors, attitudes, and confidence of someone who has already achieved what we desire, we can create positive changes in ourselves and eventually become the person we aspire to be.

The phrase "Faking It Till You Make It" doesn't imply deceit but rather a deliberate and positive approach to transforming ourselves. Like an actor immersing themselves in a role to become someone entirely different on the stage, you can adopt new habits, body language, and attitudes to transform yourself externally, thus propelling your life from "good" to "great."

## Why Fake It Till You Make it

When researching this chapter, I found that the notion of "Faking It Till You Make It" was met with mixed opinions, with some dismissing it as insincere and deceptive. After all, modern con artists capitalize on their ability to persuade people into believing something else.

However, this philosophy can be a powerful tool for personal growth and self-improvement when approached with an open mindset.

Embracing the idea of acting with conviction, as if something has already happened, to manifest a future can help you overcome self-doubt, venture into uncharted territories, and ultimately transform yourself into the confident and capable individual you aspire to be.

You might not be over the moon about where you are in life, but when we act as if we are already successful, competent, and self-assured, we send powerful signals to our subconscious mind. Whether your dream is to be an integral worker, an A+ student, or a reliable parent, realizing you can change things can help you take the first step toward that long road to greatness.

Adopting a "Fake It Till You Make It" approach can help you harness your inner self-confidence for personal growth and achievement. Consider a hypothetical example of someone starting a new job. They feel anxious and unsure, plagued by thoughts of inadequacy.

However, rather than succumbing to self-doubt, they "fake it" or act the opposite of how they feel; they act sure of themselves and confident. They dress the part, walk confidently, and engage with colleagues positively and assertively.

As they continue to project an air of competence, their interactions become more genuine, and their abilities to tackle challenges grow stronger. Over time, "faking it" becomes a natural part of their identity, and they discover that they have transformed into capable and confident professionals.

Even with fear holding you back, once you are brave enough to pretend and take that first step towards greatness, you'll rise above your limitations and propel yourself towards success. At first, it might feel fake, like you're dishonest and nothing has changed. But if you stick with your newfound persona, you'll find that your life will begin to turn around positively, like your attitude. If friends and family call you out on your path to greatness, tell them it's all part of the process.

Adopting this mindset allows us to break free from the shackles of our comfort zones. By pretending to be someone who takes risks and embraces challenges, we can venture into unexplored territories with the potential for personal growth and success. The courage to "fake it till you make it, till you believe it, till you embody it" allows us to overcome limiting beliefs, build necessary self-confidence, and discover untapped potential within ourselves.

## Overcoming Limiting Beliefs

Often, we hold ourselves back due to self-doubt and limiting beliefs. Before jumping from IT to Sales, I had minimal aspirations of doing more or being better. I was content with where I was, and while satisfaction is essential in life, it can walk a fine line with settling.

Are you delighted, or are you merely content with not failing? By "faking it," we challenge these negative thought patterns and take on a more positive and confident outlook. This practice helps break the cycle of self-sabotage and empowers us to take necessary actions.

When I switched over to sales, I expected it to be a walk in the park. I had the charisma and a natural flair for talking to people. It was meant to be all along. However, when the senior sales officer asked me to give a presentation to over 2000 colleagues, I felt like retreating into my shell.

Thankfully, as I told you in Chapter 3, I overcame the disproportionate fear of public speaking and built a new passion for the skill. Still, it's essential to note that surmounting that formidable barrier took more than one presentation.

I still struggled with the fear of public speaking for some time. Despite knowing my abilities, I occasionally felt the cold grip of nerves envelope me right before climbing the stage. However, adopting the "Faking It Till You Make It" mindset was a powerful strategy to dismantle these limiting beliefs and unlock my true capabilities.

Backed with the memory of previous presentations, I would fake the confidence I needed whenever I was afraid. Regardless of whatever that nagging voice of doubt was saying, I would face the audience, stand tall, maintain eye contact, and speak with authority.

With each presentation, I gradually realized that my overall performance was improving. As I made fewer mistakes and captivated crowds, the fear receded until my confidence was legitimate. Faking it until you make it involves consciously adopting behaviors and attitudes that challenge our self-imposed limitations and our disproportionate fears.

By pretending to be confident, capable, and "great," we defy the negative thoughts that hold us back. As we consistently act as if these beliefs do not define us, we reshape our self-perception and open ourselves up to new possibilities.

If you doubt your ability to *BeeBetter* or stand out, engage in positive behaviors that strengthen your belief in your capabilities and reinforce the idea that you can succeed. Faking it until you make it becomes a stepping stone towards genuine transformation, helping you build the confidence and self-assurance needed to achieve your goals and lead a fulfilling life.

## Adapting to Change

Life often requires us to adapt and take on new roles and responsibilities. "Faking it" allows us to step into these roles more easily and gracefully, even if we feel uncertain or unprepared.

However, it's crucial to note that growth seldom occurs within the confines of our comfort zones. If I'd remained in IT, working with systems all day would've never allowed me to become the skilled presenter I am today.

While it was tough to fight off the nerves initially, I saw it as a fundamental aspect of my personal growth and development. Life is a constant series of transitions, and our ability to navigate these changes can significantly impact our success and happiness. Embracing the mindset can be a powerful tool in helping you adapt to new situations when things change.

Feeling anxious or unsure is normal when faced with unfamiliar circumstances or challenges. But faking, acting with confidence and acting as if you are already comfortable in the new environment will signal to your subconscious mind that you can handle the change.

This reassurance helps you break free from self-doubt and fear, allowing you to approach the situation more positively and proactively. For example, if you're starting a new job in a different industry. You may be filled with doubts about your ability to perform well in an unfamiliar role or setting.

However, with the "Faking It till You Make It" approach, you choose to project confidence and competence. As you immerse yourself in the role, you'll discover that your initial apprehension begins to fade. You'll adapt to the new environment more quickly, and your actions and behavior will align with the confident persona you project. Over time, the change will become less daunting, and you will genuinely find your place within the organization.

### Creating a New Habit

Habits are formed through repetition. By repeatedly practicing positive behaviors and attitudes, we can internalize them and make them a natural part of who we are. However, if you've ever tried to pick up a new habit like exercising regularly or playing the guitar, you know it's not a walk in the park.

Carving out time in your already busy schedule and staying motivated when you fail can make it difficult to stick. But by acting as if the desired habit is ingrained in your daily routine, you can rewire your brain and build momentum toward positive change.

For example, if you want to adopt a regular exercise routine, you may need help finding motivation and consistency. However, by faking your love for the avid exercise habit, you can commit to going to the gym regularly, even when you don't like it. If you dress, eat, and behave like a physically active individual, you'll eventually see the mental and physical benefits of exercising.

The positive outcomes reinforce their commitment; they enjoy and prioritize working out. If you want to step it up a notch, refer to yourself as a gym rat, a jogger, or a yoga enthusiast. Jonah Berger, a Wharton Professor, and international best-selling author, highlighted in his latest book, Magic Words, that turning actions into identities makes people more likely to act following that label.

A 2011 study tried this experiment by sending thousands of leaflets to encourage people to vote in the coming election. In areas where the leaflets appealed to residents to be a voter, as opposed to simply asking them to vote, the voter turnout was 15% higher. You can also use this powerful approach to yourself to act as a catalyst for your outward transformation.

Instead of referring to yourself as someone trying to read more, call yourself a reader. You're already a mindful eater, rather than someone trying to adopt a new diet, and you're a gym rat instead of someone trying to exercise consistently. By consistently acting as if the desired habit is already part of our routine, we can rewire our brains and build momentum toward positive change.

Over time, the practice becomes ingrained, and what once required conscious effort becomes second nature. But remember, fake it till you make it doesn't just mean you just imagine going to the gym. You go to the gym; the faking part has to do with you acting like you like it! This is not just an exercise in tricking ourselves that we're rich and we empty our bank accounts spending like we have it.

## What Can You Do Differently Today?

Understanding that you shouldn't be quick to dismiss the "Fake It Till You Make It" approach can be liberating. It opens you up to opportunities that push you further on your path to personal growth.

By exuding confidence on the outside, you can set the stage for the positive impact that ripples into other areas of your lives, boosting productivity and overall happiness.

Two fundamental aspects of your life that will benefit from an external transformation include your body language and vocabulary: Your body language speaks volumes about your confidence and self-assurance. As you consistently practice confident body language, you start to internalize this behavior, leading to genuine boosts in self-confidence.

Others perceive you as more assertive and capable, opening doors to new opportunities and positive interactions. Also, how we communicate reflects our confidence and intelligence regarding vocabulary. Adopting a more positive vocabulary and articulate speech, even if it fakes how, you normally speak, can influence how others and we perceive ourselves. By using thoughtful and encouraging language, you can spur yourself to be more effective and persuasive in your interactions with others.

## Body Language

Let me talk about the physical. Physically, when people feel powerless, they contract, make themselves more minor, and take up less space. When approached by a foe, the image of a snail or tortoise taking cover in its shell may come to mind. On the other hand, when people feel powerful, they do the exact opposite. They expand and take up space.

Body language is a nonverbal form of communication that plays a crucial role in how we interact with others and how they perceive us. According to Albert Mehrabian, a professor of psychology, spoken words account for only 7% of communication. In comparison, your tone of voice depicts 38% of what you say, and our body language carries the bulk of all conversations by racking up an astounding 55%. In other words, your behavior matters much more than what you say.

Like animals, how we expand, or contract says much about whether we are predators or prey. Do you cross your arms nervously when you speak, or open and become expressive when approaching strangers? Have you ever paid attention to yourself when you're talking to people that have authority or just to other people in general?

How do you negotiate with your boss? Do you lazily recline your chair and then softly blurt out what you want? Or do you sit up straight and make eye contact as you outline why you deserve to get a raise? These are so minimal things that you barely pay attention to them but understanding how to effectively utilize body language can significantly improve your personal and professional relationships.

The first of many that we need to tackle is our ever-complicated facial expressions and yes, I know what you're thinking about right now and no, we're not going to do facial pushups and forehead pull ups. Facial expressions are considered as one of the primary aspects of body language and though facial experiences are the simples form of communication, they also are the strongest.

Researchers have found that smiling, even if it was fake, can bring about feelings of happiness and reduce stress. NYC based neurologist Dr. Isha Gupta claims that mere smiling can increase levels of dopamine and serotonin, our body's feel-good hormones.

When released in the body, dopamine increases feelings of happiness, and serotonin reduces stress levels while combating feelings of depression and aggression. Even though a fake smile reproduces these effects, it's worth consciously practicing positive facial expressions. Not only will faking a smile when you don't feel like smiling make you a little more likable and approachable, but it also changes your mood and gradually changes it to genuine happiness.

And when you're more positive, it's much easier to feel great. Another aspect of body language that can be a powerful tool in building rapport and fostering connections with others is your posture.

When I transitioned into sales, I was in a more customer-centric role, requiring me to pick up on physical cues quickly. I had to observe people.

Were they continuously looking at their watch? anxious to leave? or jittery from a lack of self-confidence? Whatever their body language portrayed, regardless of what they were saying, I would instantly act accordingly, whether that was keeping the conversation short or reassuring them we were on the same team. Beyond how others perceive us, body language also influences how we feel about ourselves. The "power posing" concept highlights the link between body language and our internal state.

Research suggests that assuming expansive and open postures can lead to increased feelings of confidence and reduced levels of stress hormones. By intentionally adopting power poses, we can boost our self-assurance and approach challenging situations with a more positive mindset.

Harnessing the power of body language can influence how we feel about ourselves, it can empower you to approach life's challenges with greater self-assurance and resilience. When we expand and take up space, we send a signal to our brain that we are safe, that we are great, and that we can *BeeBetter*.

## Vocabulary

In pursuing personal growth and self-improvement, adopting a positive vocabulary can be a transformative strategy under the "Faking It Till You Make It" approach. Your words reflect your thoughts and emotions and shape your perceptions and experiences. That is the fundamental message at this book's heart: consciously using positive language can influence your mindset, interactions with others, and overall outlook.

How you view life comes down to how you speak of yourself. A famous quote by Henry Ford goes, "Whether you think you can, or you think you can't, you're right".

The saying emphasizes the power of words in transforming our reality. When I worked in IT, I replied to the question, "Peter, how are you?" with "I'm fine," or simply, "Good," that's exactly what I was—mediocre and content with merely existing.

I would use self-defeating language when things weren't going my way and wallow in the misery of how unfair the world was. If you've ever found yourself saying or even thinking, "I'm no good at this," "It's not meant for people like me," or the classic "I'm a failure," then you're guilty of negative self-talk.

However, when I discovered the power of words on my self-perception, I started to make a conscious effort to beat it. We reinforce a positive self-image when using positive language to describe ourselves and our abilities. On the other hand, when we talk down on ourselves, we strengthen those limiting self-beliefs. For instance, instead of saying, *"I'm not good at this,"* adopting the phrase, *"I am improving every day,"* shifts our perspective from self-doubt to growth and progress.

These positive affirmations can build self-confidence and motivate us to strive for our goals. As your confidence grows, it'll feel more authentic when you say, *"I'm great at this."* Adopting a positive vocabulary also profoundly impacts our interactions with others.

Using words of encouragement and appreciation can uplift and inspire those around us. We strengthen our connections and foster a supportive and uplifting environment when we genuinely compliment others and express gratitude for their efforts. After hearing my buzzword, I can't count how many people have reconsidered talking or working with me.

Something about responding enthusiastically, especially on cloudy days, gets people curious. Positive language can create a ripple effect, spreading positivity and fostering a sense of camaraderie among friends, family, and colleagues.

So, even if you *"fake"* a positive vocabulary consistently, it becomes a part of you. Consistently choosing your words will cultivate a more optimistic and empowering outlook. By consciously choosing positive and empowering words to challenge these limiting beliefs, we can break free from their hold and unleash our true potential.

## Balancing Authenticity

Balancing authenticity with a little bit of *"faking it till you make it"* is a delicate yet essential aspect of navigating social interactions and personal growth. Authenticity refers to being true to yourself and expressing genuine emotions, beliefs, and values. On the other hand, being fake involves adopting behaviors or attitudes that do not align with one's true self, often to fit in or gain approval from others. I do not advocate for the latter when I outline the benefits of *"faking it till you make it"* or highlighting what areas of your life might benefit most from a tune-up.

On the contrary, I encourage you to be your most authentic self. After all, authenticity is the foundation of meaningful connections and relationships. When we are genuine, we invite trust and vulnerability, enabling others to connect with us on a deeper level.

Throughout this chapter, I use the phrase "Fake It Till You Make It" to adapt and grow in social settings or professional environments. In certain situations, adopting social norms or adjusting one's behavior to fit in can facilitate smoother interactions and foster harmony within groups.

It emphasizes adopting the attitude and behavior of the person you wish to become, a superior version of yourself. However, it is essential to balance authenticity and social adaptability. For example, even when I am nervous, I would exert effort to showcase confidence and assertiveness during my public presentations.

Over time, consistently leaving a positive impression on my audience changed my mindset, about public speaking. I'm no longer battling stage fright; I'm a confident presenter who can captivate crowds on any stage.

When your external transformations align with your authentic self, it ultimately leads to a more fulfilling life. While it may seem *"fake"* initially, presenting the best version of yourself in various social contexts allows you to remain faithful while excelling in other capacities.

Finding the balance between authenticity and "faking it till you make it" is a dynamic process that requires self-awareness and adaptability. Striking this balance allows us to be true to ourselves while adapting appropriately to different contexts.

The key is to remain authentic and continue live by our core values and beliefs while remaining open to individual growth, learning new things, and creating positive social interactions by gradually mastering how to balance authenticity, we can build deeper connections and embrace our true selves without compromising our individuality.

## Embracing External Change

It's important to note that "Fake It till You Make It" is not about being dishonest or insincere. It's a tool for personal growth and transformation, emphasizing the power of mindset and action. The goal is to align our outward behavior with our inner aspirations and to continue growing until the changes become genuine and natural.

As you evolve and gain more confidence through your efforts, you gradually become the person you aspire to be, embodying the qualities that were once "faked until they were made."

*"Faking It Till You Make It"* is a potent approach to change that can empower us to embrace personal greatness. By altering our outward behavior and mindset, we pave the way for profound internal transformation. As we learn to embody our desired qualities, we discover the strength to create positive, lasting change. The power of transformation lies within us, waiting to be unlocked by the courage to embrace change and the commitment to become the best versions of ourselves.

"Fake it till you make it" represents the process, the courage to adopt new thoughts, words, and actions, despite their unfamiliar tax on us, until we embody the change we seek. Embracing external change empowers us to become the best versions of ourselves and unlock our full potential for a more fulfilling and successful life. While it might be hard to take that first step towards being a dedicated student, an innovative entrepreneur, or a consistent gym goer, pretending you already are is a powerful approach to achieving your goals. By "faking it till we make" our way to external change, we can overcome self-doubt and transform our lives positively.

So, let us dare to pretend, step into our greatness, and realize the incredible potential that lies within us.

## Chapter 6

**A Little Gratitude Goes A Long Way**

Have you ever noticed how some people shine with happiness, even when life gets tough? It might be a friend who seems to bounce back quickly in the face of adversity or a co-worker who never complains, no matter how heavy the workload gets. Whoever it is, I'm willing to bet if you take a closer look at their lives, you'll find that their secret is gratitude.

Gratitude means being thankful for the things in your life, big or small. In pursuing personal growth and transformation, few tools wield as much power as gratitude. A study by Harvard Medical School shows that grateful people are more likely to experience positive emotions. So, knowing how going from "good," to "great" can transform your life, it makes sense to embrace gratitude as a way of life.

The more grateful you are, the more likely you are to adopt a new buzzword, feel more fulfilled with your life, and achieve success. After all, when you're more enthusiastic about life, it's easier and feels more authentic when you say, "I'm great, excellent, or buzzing."

However, I know that counting your blessings is not always easy. Harboring feelings of resentment, jealousy, or betrayal can make it a lot harder to be grateful. Early on in my career, I had to battle these emotions, and it was hard for me to remain in a positive place at that point in my development. One of the most notable examples that comes to mind is when I delved into real estate. Before I started my corporate job at ATC, I needed another income source.

From my experience working at a computer store, I'd gotten connected with a much younger but incredibly gifted programmer, Jason, and we'd developed some high-tech software for the real estate market. We called it the 'Talk 2' app, and it was designed to allow potential renters and homebuyers to communicate with the owner during virtual tours. It was a unique solution to improve the virtual home viewing experience, and considering it was the early 2000s, it had a lot of growth potential.

Despite having an excellent product, neither Jason nor I had much experience with the real estate world, and it was a ton of work trying to make a pitch.

I knew if we wanted to make it, our best bet to break into the market would be through someone with an already established reputation laying the groundwork for us.

So, leveraging my networking and socialization skills, I approached one of my contacts, Robert "Bobby" Dawson.

"Bobby" was in his late 40s to early 50s, had the charm of a veteran actor, and was well-known in the real estate world. He was the ideal person we needed to open doors for us. Bobby quickly became my mentor and was instrumental in pushing the 'Talk 2' app forward.

Thanks to our newfound partnership, Jason and I finally made some money off our project. It was the perfect match for our budding company, and everyone had their defined role. Jason handled the technical aspects, I dealt with the billing, and Robert tapped into his extensive network to get us more customers.

'Talk 2' was one of the first companies I launched, and for the company to have a reasonable amount of success in the early days put me on cloud 9. Despite leaving the assurance of a 9-5 job, I was earning a stable income, and although it wasn't at the top of my mind, I was grateful. And it was easy to be positive until it wasn't.

After a couple of years, Jason and I realized we'd been duped. Unbeknownst to us, my mentor, "Bobby", had gotten a consulting gig with another company and took everything he'd learned from us and sold it. Despite dedicating so much time, sweat, and money to building 'Talk 2' from the ground up, it no longer belonged to me.

Robert sold the IP to another company without my or Jason's approval, and we didn't have a dime to show for it. Being more established, the other company was able to quickly develop and launch a replica of our product, claiming our long-term clients and pushing us out of the market in no time. While 'Talk 2' imploded, "Bobby" comfortably grinned as he counted his money. I hated him.

My hatred for "Bobby" weighed on me like a ton of bricks for five years, and I carried it everywhere. As I launched other businesses, it followed me.

When I started my own family, it stayed with me. It may not have been at the forefront of my mind, but it lingered just below the surface and occasionally resurfaced to ruin my mood.

In hindsight, I wonder why I let it stay with me for so long. I'd bounced back and successfully created other companies. I wasn't in a financial rot doomed to go hungry because of one man's greed. But I continued to let my hatred ruin several great days after that encounter.

Eventually, I realized my hatred for Robert was doing more harm than good, and I had to let it go. I decided to make peace five years after he'd swindled Jason and me. I planned to move to Utah and wanted my conscience clear—a fresh start with a new mind.

At the time, "Bobby" was still very active in the real estate scene, so locating him wasn't difficult. I showed up at one of his open houses, and he was shocked to see me. Although I'd carried him with me for the last five years, we'd never exchanged a word since we parted ways after 'Talk 2' crumbled.

I'm not sure what must've been going through his head then, but he agreed when I asked if we could talk at a local coffee shop. I explained that I'd held a grudge against him for a while and realized I needed to forgive him to move on with my life. Although I'd done it solely for my benefit, it briefly occurred to me that "Bobby" might be remorseful. He wasn't.

If anything, he seemed surprised and blissfully unaware that he'd done anything malicious worth bearing a grudge for five years. It would've been understandable for me to flare up.

After all, I'd dedicated a considerable amount of time in the last few years to resenting this man for something that had probably never crossed his mind. But at that point, I was over it. I'd realized hating him wasn't worth it. The negativity wasn't worth it.

Was it easy? Heck, no. It took me five years, approximately 1825 days, to get over it. I lost countless hours and months. Outside of that, I was unhappy and bitter, while the person who offended me had long moved on with his life. Who knows how long I would've continued to harbor feelings of loathing if I hadn't adopted a "great" attitude?

It was difficult for me to fully step into my newfound mindset to be *"great"* when "Bobby" still held me back, so I knew I had to forgive him. It can be hard to let go if you're mauling over someone or something that's cheated you in the past. But you must realize you're letting whatever hurt you continue to wield power over you in the present.

Whether it's a former lover who's moved on and started a new family or a job that laid you off after taking years of your life, you must move on. And being grateful allows you to embrace a more positive outlook, making achieving inner peace easier.

That's why this chapter is so essential to this book. Gratitude is more than just a fleeting emotion; it is a potent mindset shift that propels us from the realm of "good" to "great." Our journey to *BeeBetter* wouldn't be complete without exploring the profound impact of embracing gratitude and how it can reshape our lives.

In this chapter, we will uncover the science behind gratitude's effects on our well-being and its role in self-transformation, relationships, and the world around us, and learn how gratitude can be harnessed to overcome challenges and adversity.

## Gratitude and Attitude

At its core, gratitude is all about noticing and liking the things in our lives. It's about saying, "Hey, thanks for that!" to the good stuff and people around us. This basic idea of appreciation is the base that makes gratitude so powerful. Gratitude is more than a mere polite gesture or a fleeting emotion. It's a mindset that affects how we see the world. Looking for moments in your life that make you think, "Wow, my life is awesome!" is what having an attitude of gratitude is all about.

Adopting an attitude of gratitude can even have positive benefits for your physical well-being. Psychologist Shelley Taylor proved in her study of Breast Cancer patients that those with a more optimistic outlook, "positive illusions," as she termed it, in their circumstance were more likely to have better mental health, lower mortality rates, and better biological response to their treatment.

Her incredible results demonstrate how being grateful can impact your health. In this instance, patients with a "great" mindset found that their bodies followed suit.

As many of us have discovered, sometimes all the positiveness in the world does not triumph over physical illness, we are mortal. A wonderful friend of mine, a young man who grew up with Cerebral Palsy, who lived in pain and discomfort all his short life taught me a great lesson. One day he had told me how he really liked this girl in our neighborhood, and how he sometimes felt saddened that he could never directly have that type of experience in his life, but he said, perhaps no other human can experience the joy of loving the idea of a romance this much without any hope that they will love you back.

He sighed and said, "I feel so grateful." Many years after his death, I feel grateful for his gift. He was my hero.

A famous quote by John Lubbock goes, "What we see depends mainly on what we look for." It's not uncommon for us to view the world with a pessimistic lens. The news and media are rife with catastrophic and horrifying stories that urge us to believe the worst of humanity and expect the worst from the world.

Our eyes focus on what is wrong and zone in on the negative, allowing us to miss the parts of our lives that are "great." Looking at the bigger picture instead of focusing on the bad can open us up to a more positive experience. Other researchers support Taylor's conclusion, including Sonya Lyubormirski and Karl Tucker, who looked into the difference between happy and unhappy people.

Sonya and Karl trained participants to see new scenarios positively in their study. At the end of their experiment, they found the participants experienced greater positive emotions and lower anxiety levels, making them happier than their more pessimistic counterparts.

Deciding to look at what we already have instead of what we don't changes everything in our lives. From our mindset to our health, gratitude helps us see things more positively and feel thankful. We become the designers of our happiness, creating a better and brighter reality.

## Gratitude and Abundance

I decided to include this as a sub-section because, in our world, many of us attach our worth to how much we earn. Many consider money a symbol of abundance, allowing it to dictate how grateful or ungrateful we feel. We often let our next paycheck, how well our business is going, or if we win the lottery determine our outlook. But applying rose-tinted glasses to our financial lives can unlock new perspectives on wealth and prosperity.

Still, looking on the bright side of things can often be challenging when we live in a world seemingly driven by money. People spend their entire lives and sometimes lose it while chasing wealth. So, there are a lot of emotions surrounding money. Whether you're indifferent, feel like capitalism is the root of evil, or are desperate to simply put food on the table, money triggers strong emotions. So when we don't examine our priorities, it can feel like we're stuck in an endless rat race because the money will never be enough.

Consider how excited Jeff Bezos, the multi-billionaire founder of Amazon, might be if he wins a million-dollar lottery. It would barely be a pebble on top of his massive mountain of wealth. If you start at the bottom of the corporate ladder, earning $35,000 a year, a raise to $50,000 may be exciting in the first few months. You could move to a nicer apartment, change your wardrobe, and treat your friends and family to lovely gifts. But after a while, that would adjust to your norm, and earning that *much* money would no longer excite you. And if your income were to go up again, the cycle would repeat itself till you were as numb as Jeff Bezos might be to earning a million.

With that said, does that mean it's all pointless? On the contrary, money can be a powerful vehicle for unlocking spectacular experiences. But that's the thing. You need to view it as the vehicle and not the destination.

Suppose you're a person filled with the intense spirit of wanderlust. You'd like to see the pyramids of Egypt, walk along the beaches of Santorini, and see the Southern Lights in Antarctica.

Having a loaded wallet could help you quickly achieve all these, but there are many ways to travel on a budget. Looking for a job overseas, volunteering, and travel networks can help you satisfy your dream of vacationing in another country.

So, while money can be a luxury vehicle, many others exist. And that's why I always tell my daughter to chase happiness, not money. True abundance isn't a measure of what you have. It's how you make the most of what you already have.

Early in life, I'd piqued an interest in computers, so naturally, when I was ready to join the workforce, it made sense to work on what I loved. Thankfully, I found a job at a computer store with an owner willing to saddle me with as much responsibility as I wanted. But what I loved the most about working at that store was Kyle, my co-worker. He was a computer enthusiast like me, and together, we turned a lot of profit buying wholesale parts, customizing them, and reselling them.

When we were ready to move on, his mom helped us land our first corporate jobs at a telecommunication company. We were earning around $9 an hour, and I was content because I got to do what I loved all day. At that point, my plan wasn't to become rich overnight. It was to work my way up from making computers to training others who shared my passion.

Knowing my priorities, I eagerly scouted for an opening to give me the upward mobility I craved to achieve my dreams. So, when I landed a job at ATC, I knew I was on the right track. Kyle and I would often compare notes, as young professionals often do, and in the first year, we were earning around $30,000. We were equals in that regard, but only for a short time.

While I craved stability and an environment that would let me flourish, Kyle wanted to climb the corporate ladder quickly and start earning big bucks. He'd always been brilliant, and it was no surprise he landed a job at IBM, making around $120,000. In other words, he would start earning four times what I was earning at IT support in ATC.

It was a huge jump, and I considered doing the same as I helped my friend pack up his life and begin again in the US. But as tempting as the money was, I decided to stay put. I was happy with my job and knew it was where I needed to be to grow in the direction I wanted in the long run. A few years down the road, I stood in line with our VP, Jean, and he would ask me a question that would change the trajectory of my life.

In retrospect, I'm grateful I have a tangible moment I can recall when I told my daughter to choose happiness over money. By creating an external marker for success and wanting to grow in IT, I didn't feel the need to compare myself with Kyle. Although I was making less money, I still felt an abundance in my life. If you're stuck up on how your friends or your colleagues are making more money than you, chances are high you're going to feel unsatisfied with your life.

Even if you can dig deep and earn up to or more than the person, you're comparing yourself to guess what? There'll still be someone with a fatter paycheck. The solution to escaping the mental rat race is to find many sources of fulfillment.

Even if you can dig deep and earn up to or more than the person, you're comparing yourself to guess what? There'll still be someone with a fatter paycheck. The solution to escaping the mental rat race is to find many sources of fulfillment.

Ask yourself, besides money, what else do you want to achieve? Do you want to go back to school and earn a degree? Finish that online course you started but always procrastinate? Or maybe you want to get through the day without losing your temper?

Creating your metrics for success allows you to stop defaulting to the automatic societal narrative that if you're not making more money, you're failing because you are not. When you cultivate gratitude for your current resources and how much progress you've made with your goals, you reframe your perception of wealth. It becomes easier to recognize that true abundance is rooted in contentment.

## Gratitude and Relationships

Connecting with s these connections even stronger; It takes regular, everyday conversations and turns them into something significant. When we say "thank you" to the people around us, we tell them we appreciate what they do. Gratitude does something unique in our relationships.

It's like tossing a pebble into a pond, creating a ripple effect of positive emotions.

So, when you genuinely say "thanks," it can make both you and the other person feel "great." It's like being the type of person who appreciates others for the big and little things. And that could be as simple as a polite word of appreciation when the barista adds an extra pump of milk to your coffee or buying a heartfelt gift for a coworker going out of their way to help with a project.

Gratitude isn't just something you show on the outside; it's like a warm, fuzzy feeling on the inside that makes our conversations real and full of kindness. My grandmother died at the grand age of 99 years old.

Although she lived a great life, knowing she was no longer with us, still hurts me. She has always been a constant through many milestones in my life, and it wasn't easy to picture a world without her. Since I was a kid, my grandmother has always supported me at every stage.

When I was a child and told her I wanted to buy a house, rather than laugh at my juvenile innocence, she'd reassured me I could buy one when I was older. She even followed up by teaching me about money and how to budget when I started working multiple jobs at 14. I'd gained my first morsel of independence when I moved out of my parent's house and stayed with her.

My grandmother gave me room to figure out life as an adult. As an adult, I leaned on her support, and with her advice and financial contribution, I could buy my first house as she'd promised all those years ago. She established the foundation of my financial knowledge, setting me up for success early on amidst beloved hugs and kisses, and suddenly, she was no more.

Newspaper editor Roeliff Brinkerhoff once said, "Funerals are for the living." They're a way for mourners to acknowledge the reality of death and allow them to express grief and loss with support. At my grandmother's funeral, I reflected on her life and her significant role in mine. I was sad at that moment, realizing I couldn't talk to her anymore. Looking at her picture and thinking about everything and how I'd miss her filled me with grief. When my emotions eventually erupted in a flood, my daughter wrapped her arms around me to comfort me. It helped that some people shared the same feelings and could extend some level of grace and compassion.

Letting go of my emotions with people that I love and cared for around me, made the entire ordeal a little more bearable. Although the day had started gloomy, my family shared stories about how my grandmother had impacted our lives and what she'd taught us over the years. Some of the stories were heartfelt, and others were funny, but they all helped keep her memory alive.

Although I was grieving because of my grandmother's passing, I was also grateful I could hold on to all the memories we shared together. You can experience genuine appreciation for the human connections you've formed through rose-tinted glasses.

If you've experienced the trauma of losing a loved one, you can relate to how painful it can be and how its finality can seem so unfair. My friend Lynette understands this completely, having lost her parents, her father just this year, and her mother 10 years ago.

After being diagnosed with Multiple Sclerosis, Lynette's mother went from frequently hiking the Lake District in England, fostering children, and working in a nursery to being a wheelchair user. She spent her last days in a nursing home with other residents, typically 20 years her senior. Naturally, her mother's death upset Lynette, but it also allowed her to grow.

Knowing that life can turn upside down at any moment made it important to appreciate the little things. Talking about that shared experience with Lynette resonated with me deeply. It made me laugh as my mom popped into my head, immediately reminding me of a silly song she used to sing.

With a tear in her eye, she would grin and tilt her head from side to side in time with the music, singing, "Always look on the bright side of life."

Following my grandmother's funeral, I didn't feel "great," but I didn't want to dwell on all the negatives after allowing myself to express it. Instead of sinking into despair, I made it a point to focus on what would make things better.

With her passing, I realized how vital memories were. Being able to share stories and lessons I'd learned from her made me want to recreate inspired by hers my own memorable life.

That year, I told myself I would do more traveling. I wanted to go to the Caribbean islands with my family or somewhere we'd never been. After all, life is like a big, colorful quilt, and we add a new thread whenever we go through good or challenging times with people.

Gratitude is looking at every joyful or challenging interaction like an extra thread. It helps us see our relationships positively and shows how even tough moments can be a source of connection.

Life is a lot like a photo album, the wonderful moments caught and frozen in time live on visually, the album itself, the pages and the covers represent all the life that happens around, over, and in between and "glues" the moments we choose to memorialize in the photos into a full life.

"Life is a lot like a photo album, the wonderful moments caught and frozen in time…"

Peter Bradford

# Gratitude and Challenges

Lynette had a breakthrough while we were writing this chapter. She went to bed with the day's thoughts swirling in her head. But she quieted her mind and focused on what she wanted to achieve. Lynette understood when actively trying to visualize life with a rosy hue, the shadow of a dark cloud would encroach and put a downer on any situation.

Acknowledging the cloud and accepting it was there, without brushing it away thoughtlessly, enabled her to visualize herself pushing the dark cloud away with strength in her heart. Instead of focusing on the negative thoughts in her head, Lynette would concentrate on what made her happy.

So, when the sky turned grey, Lynette's heart grew bigger, pushing it away. After several battles between light and darkness, the cloud stopped being insistent. Through learned behavior, it was starting to give up, making each day more manageable. Sometimes, on the road to being great, we face challenging times that test our strength and determination. Gratitude helps us a lot during these challenging times.

Although it doesn't make the problems disappear, it gives us a reason to keep going and stay strong. It's like having a secret power that helps us look on the bright side and keep hope alive, no matter how hard things get.

# How to Remain Grateful

**Stay in the Present:**

One of the best things about gratitude is its ability to anchor us to the present. Getting caught up in a web of past regrets and future anxieties is easy in a fast-paced world. But practicing mindfulness by staying fully present in each moment can help us appreciate the simple moments. Instead of dwelling on what has passed or worrying about what lies ahead, you should focus on the blessings and experiences that grace us now.

When Lynette discovered this truth, she could stay positive, recalling the "loving-kindness" meditation she had once tried on a Buddhist retreat. Staying present in the moment and paying attention to your surroundings, feelings, and the people around you can help you pursue greatness through gratitude.

**Wear Rose-Colored Glasses:**

Reprogramming yourself with more positive intentions starts in your mind. Your actions will change when your views, perceptions, and feelings change. Try to adopt a positive outlook on life. Instead of dwelling on problems, focus on solutions and the good things in your life. See challenges as opportunities for growth. In Chapter 2, I highlighted how rock bottom can be a tool for propulsion. Gratitude can also allow you to see setbacks as springboards for better things.

**Embrace Self-Growth:**

Understand that personal growth often comes from overcoming difficulties. So when you embrace challenges as chances to learn, you develop resilience, and you're more likely to be grateful when good things finally happen.

Remember that you don't have to wait for the big things to celebrate. Each step forward should be a reason to be grateful. Whenever Lynette could focus on positive thoughts, wake up without complaining, and get on her feet when needed, it was a win and a step further away from the dark.

**Rediscover Your Childlike Wonder:**

I admire children because they can find wonder and joy in the simplest things. Somewhere along the journey, this capacity often fades as we become adults. Think about how excited kids get at having ice cream after a meal or repeatedly listening to the same song.

Thankfully, gratitude can reignite our childlike wonder, infusing our lives with newfound positivity. Lynette encourages her children to race raindrops down the window of their motorhome and dance in the rain on the beach, humming the tune, "I'm singing in the rain," to her gleeful kids.

When cultivating gratitude intentionally, we train our minds to focus on the small marvels surrounding us daily. A clear sky, a warm cup of tea, and a kind word from a friend, seemingly small moments become a source of gratitude, returning us to our childlike, appreciative nature.

Try to reconnect with that childlike curiosity and enthusiasm for life. It can help you see the world with fresh eyes and appreciate its beauty.

**Get a Journal:**

A powerful tool in the journey of gratitude is a gratitude journal. Through the simple act of recording daily moments of gratitude, we can create a well of positivity. Research in positive psychology confirms that reflecting on our blessings can rewire our brains, facilitating a more optimistic outlook.

Over time, this practice becomes a natural response, making looking on the bright side easier whenever life happens. Journaling can also be a mode of self-reflection. When I decided I needed to spread the message of this book, that one word can change your life, it was essential for me to reflect on my life thus far.

Thinking back on my stories, I could be grateful for how much selecting an enthusiastic buzzword had transformed my life. My journal entries proved that everyone could adopt a more positive, appreciative mindset and *BeeBetter*.

Consider keeping a journal where you write down things, you're grateful for daily. It could be as simple as a sunny day, a good meal, or a kind word from a friend. Writing them down reinforces your sense of gratitude.

"Try to reconnect with that childlike curiosity and enthusiasm for life. It can help you see the world with fresh eyes and appreciate its beauty."

Peter Bradford

## Chapter 7

### Feeding off Your Positivity

At an early age, Stephen Hawking developed an interest in the vast expanse of the cosmos. He'd been lucky enough to discover his passion quite early and was endlessly curious about how galaxies and stars came to be.

By age 21, he'd already obtained a PhD and was keen on making waves in theoretical physics, if his clumsiness would allow anyway. Stephen had always been clumsy. When he started his BA degree at Oxford, he'd always manage to trip at the most inconvenient time and would struggle to hold the chalk in his hand as he solved complex mathematical equations on a blackboard. Unfortunately, his frequent stumbles weren't a cute quirk like the protagonist in a rom-com.

By the time he'd earned his Ph.D., his clumsiness was more pronounced, and he would sometimes fall over entirely for no reason. Stephen later discovered that his 'quirk' was an early warning sign of amyotrophic lateral sclerosis-ALS.

As a degenerative motor neuron condition, ALS interferes with the body's ability to control muscles, eventually worsening until the patient becomes paralyzed. Diagnosed at 21, Stephen was decades younger than the average ALS patient, often around 55. Considering the average life expectancy for people with this condition from the time of diagnosis is 2-5 years, his situation looked bleak.

With no known cure, Stephen faced the grim possibility of dying before he could accomplish his goals. The disease slowly stole away his ability to move and speak, trapping him in a body that seemed to betray his brilliant mind. But Stephen refused to be confined by his circumstances.

With sheer determination and a relentless spirit, Stephen embraced his changing reality. Knowing his condition wouldn't deter his intelligence, he continued his scientific explorations. And even though his body grew weaker, eventually confining him to a wheelchair and necessitating the need for a computerized speech synthesizer to speak, his mind only grew sharper. He continued to pursue his passion, working on blackholes, and challenging the nature of the universe as we understood it. In 1988, 25 years after his diagnosis, he published his findings on the cosmos in a book titled,

"A Brief History of Time." Stephen Hawking's legacy inspires millions worldwide, not only for his stellar accomplishments in science but also for his unrelenting positivity through the most uncertain times.

His story is the perfect example of the transformative power of a positive mindset in the face of profound change. Despite his challenges and the progression of his illness, his determination to be "great" helped him break barriers. He once said, "My advice to other disabled people would be to concentrate on things your disability doesn't prevent you from doing well and don't regret the things it interferes with. Don't be disabled in spirit as well as physically."

Life is a series of ever-shifting landscapes with people and situations constantly shifting, much like how seasons change. Every day, we experience life's highs and lows, and staying positive is crucial throughout this journey. Being positive doesn't just make us feel better; it also positively impacts the people we interact with. Think of it like how Stephen Hawking's incredible ideas helped us understand the universe better. In the same way, our positivity can guide us toward greatness, even when we encounter inconvenient changes. In this chapter, we'll dive into how maintaining a positive mindset while dealing with twists and turns can transform our lives.

## The Dynamics of Change

Change is an intrinsic part of life that sweeps us along its course, whether we're ready to go with the flow or not. People come and go, relationships evolve, and careers experience lulls. All these changes can cause uncertainties when we experience a turning point. After working in sales for 10 years, I decided to leave the corporate world and venture into business development. One of the first and most successful companies I established, Trendy Tactics, was born out of the need to help small to medium-sized businesses generate traffic in a growing digital market.

My team of five employees and I were lucky to hit the ground running, generating significant traction in our first year. But beyond the money, what I loved about Trendy Tactics was the culture.

Our company felt like a family, as we held our staff to less rigid corporate structures. Ensuring my employees had the freedom to take time off when needed was essential to me, and it helped us grow because everyone was a lot happier with the system.

Unfortunately, you can't run a company of five the way you would a corporation of 100. When it was time for us to start scaling up, I knew things would have to change, and if we weren't tactful about it, our core values would change, too. Of course, finding people that fit our scene took a lot of work. In the beginning, I hired many wrong people who took advantage of the freedom they could get at the expense of the company's goals.

Scaling up was more difficult than I'd initially anticipated, and I had to bring in help in the form of Cameroon. Cameroon came in as our lead for operations and sales, and with his experience working with big corporations, he brought fresh ideas and tuned them to our needs. Leaning on his expertise, we had to adjust our interview style to allow us to pinpoint the right candidates.

Instead of prioritizing education and experience, I was more particular about finding competent people who fit the company culture. It took us 3 years to figure out who was best for the team, and there were certainly growing pains along the way. I also had to make some concessions, but I was adamant about Trendy Tactics retaining the feeling of a family rather than a soulless corporation.

I wanted everyone to feel "great" in the morning when they got out of bed and came to work. Sure, it meant an occasional dip in our numbers and learning some lessons the hard way, but I was satisfied knowing we'd figured out how to create a healthy working environment as a growing company. Change can make the world seem as if it's spinning on its head, disrupting our sense of stability.

Growing a business, developing an illness, or hitting a roadblock can be difficult transition periods. However, reacting with negativity or resistance can lead to unnecessary suffering and hinder our ability to adapt.

If I'd cracked down on all the staff at Trendy Tactics because a few rotten eggs had abused their liberty, the company would've changed at its core. I would've betrayed my original vision, and many of the star players we have today would've looked for a better fit. Embracing change with positivity can turn what might seem like chaos into an opportunity for renewal and growth.

## Navigating Change with Positivity

Remaining positive amidst change is not about denying the challenges or glossing over the difficulties. I know firsthand that looking on the bright side can be difficult when everything seems to be working against you. As you already know, my divorce was a rough patch. With my marriage disintegrating and my ex-wife making plans to move with our daughter to a different state, things were tense.

My family began to change rapidly, and I felt I had little say. My ex-wife and I had always had our differences, especially about how to raise Emma, and with the growing distance, it was harder for us to see eye to eye.

It was a high-stress scenario that compromised my health as I developed a hormonal imbalance, requiring medication.

Of course, my well-being wasn't helped by the restrictions on how and when I could communicate with Emma. Besides the obvious physical limitation of living across borders, talking about the past or anything related to Emma's childhood was strictly off the table when her mother was present.

While I reassured my daughter, we'd had great times when she was a kid, I was keenly aware I was walking on eggshells, which was unsettling.

Eventually, I knew something had to give. I'd always wanted to be a fantastic father, and while I had to parent under different circumstances than I'd imagined, I knew I had to do it properly anyway. I didn't want Emma to feel caught in the middle, having to choose sides. Knowing I had to think long-term, I swallowed my pride and sought to build a more positive relationship with Emma's mom.

Determined not to let things escalate, I started to adopt better ways to communicate with my ex-wife. Over time, I learned how to avoid rough conversations. I won't respond rashly when I receive a text concerning Emma. I keyed in that it was easier to avoid misunderstandings by choosing to talk rather than text.

It wasn't a straight line, and we never became besties, but with time, we both grew to understand each other, which helped us respond more tactfully. With an open mind, it was easier to embrace the changing dynamics of our relationship and be more respectful in our conversations.

"I keyed in that it was easier to avoid misunderstandings by choosing to talk rather than text." – Peter Bradford

Ultimately, it also helped Emma adjust to our reality, knowing she could always count on us to put her first. Besides, removing the negativity that came with the constant disagreements made it easier for me to stay positive and feel "great" as I made my way up from rock bottom.

Despite how unwanted or unsettling change can be, it can also be a catalyst for transformation if you let it. Cultivating a mindset that sees every shift as a chance to learn, evolve, and thrive can help you make the most of your situation when life doesn't go according to plan. So, when adapting to life after a big reset, remember that positivity can be a powerful tool to steer through the currents of change and come out "awesome."

## Stay Positive in the Face of Change

### Envision a Brighter Future:

If you've seen the 2014 biographical drama about Stephen Hawking, 'The Theory of Everything,' starring Eddie Redmayne, you might have been awe-struck as the actor portraying the English physicist turns to his doctor after receiving his ALS diagnosis and asks, "What about the brain?"

Stephen's primary concern was his work, even with the likelihood of death knocking on his door. He could've easily slipped into depression, allowing his illness to paralyze him physically and mentally (no one would've blamed him). Yet, despite the odds, he triumphed, living several decades beyond his estimated prognosis, and even outliving the doctor who'd initially diagnosed him.

Rather than limiting himself to what his condition took from him, Stephen imagined a brighter future. Even amidst the uncertainty of change, he focused on the potential outcome of his research.

He found hope in an otherwise bleak set of circumstances. This optimistic outlook can guide you through the transitional phase of an abrupt change, allowing you to make the most of new opportunities. Sometimes, it's all about choosing your angle. Take, for example, a model shot by two different photographers.

The first photographer is a professional who takes their work seriously, looking for the best angle and lighting to highlight the model's best features. They even go the distance by adding special effects to make their pictures a work of art and their muse. On the other hand, you have another less detailed photographer, taking shots with poor lighting and from unflattering angles that do little justice to the model.

Undoubtedly, the two photographers will have starkly different results thanks to how they chose to view the same model through their lenses.

Like the first photographer, envisioning a brighter, greater future can help you view your situation differently, allowing you to create more vibrant and colorful moments.

**Prioritize Self-Care:**

When the world around us shifts, it's easy to become overwhelmed. Prioritizing self-care becomes crucial during times of change. After all, when you look great, you feel great. In 2008, the American Journal of Lifestyle Medicine published findings by Schure et al. that demonstrated that self-care practices, including physical activity, proper nutrition, and sufficient sleep, were positively correlated with enhanced well-being and life satisfaction.

So, treat yourself when you can. Engaging in activities that nourish our physical, emotional, and mental well-being helps us look at the bright side. Whether exercising, meditating, spending time in nature, or enjoying a hobby, self-care provides the foundation for our positive mindset to flourish.

**Turn off Your Gadgets:**

In a world of digital distractions, constant connectivity can impede our ability to embrace change with a positive mindset. Technology is an excellent tool for facilitating conversations, making our homes and work more efficient, and bringing us closer together.

As someone who worked in IT and still works in marketing and business development, I understand how social media has changed the landscape by making communication more straightforward and faster.

However, it also has its drawbacks. With entertainment a single tap away, many people use it as a distraction when the world gets too real. Thanks to an ever-evolving algorithm that seeks to keep you glued to your phones, continuous exposure to negative news, social media comparisons, and online conflict can increase anxiety and stress and even trigger symptoms of depression. Constant screen use can also reduce mindfulness and hinder your ability to fully participate in real-life interactions and engage with your loved ones.

I recently read that a school in the UK had to put up a sign that said something like, "Get off your phone! You are picking up your child, and they are happy to see you. Show them you are happy to see them too - Please!"

Striking a balance between living in the modern world and occasionally turning off your gadgets can improve overall well-being and make coping easier when people or situations change. Research by the Journal of Social and Clinical Psychology indicated that limiting social media use to about 30 minutes daily significantly reduced depression and loneliness. Engaging in offline activities like sports, journaling, or other hobbies can help you embrace your existence and feel more grateful.

"In a world of digital distractions, constant connectivity can impede our ability to embrace change with a positive mindset." – Peter Bradford

Taking breaks from gadgets and screens allows us to disconnect from the constant stream of information and engage more deeply with our thoughts and emotions. This practice fosters self-awareness, enabling us to navigate change from a centered and positive standpoint.

**Check Your Language:**

During my time in sales, I had the opportunity to network with several professionals nationwide. With my fear of public speaking waning, it became an excellent icebreaker at events, and I would perk up whenever someone asked about my presentation or complimented me.

One of the first friends I made was a woman named Maya; she'd been present at my first presentation (the one that had me shaking in my boots) and was pleasantly surprised I'd recently hopped over from IT. "I'm not sure I could've done that," she joked.

"I'm sure you'd be great," I reassured her, to which she snorted, obviously full of doubt. Maya had always been a skeptic when it came to change. "If it ain't broke, don't fix it," had always been her mantra, making her averse to adopting a new status quo. She always felt overwhelmed and resistant whenever her boss assigned her a new role, or she had to travel for work.

Like most of us, she would mutter, "I'm fine," when someone asked how she was doing, never realizing the impact of those seemingly harmless words.

I shared with Maya how my newfound attitude and buzzword had helped me overcome my stage fright, and she resonated with it. "What have you got to lose by trying?" I asked, urging her to try it as well. I wouldn't hear from her till months later at another sales seminar.

Ultimately, I was the one complimenting her on doing an excellent job. "Thank you," Maya said enthusiastically after her presentation.

"You know Peter, it worked." After our conversation months ago, she'd felt a spark of hope and decided to try it. She practiced replacing her usual negative phrases with more positive ones for weeks.

Instead of saying, "I'm fine," she began saying, "I'm awesome," and she soon began to feel it too. Shortly after, her boss announced a significant restructuring at work, and instead of feeling anxious, Maya saw it as an opportunity to learn new skills and connect with new colleagues. She even applied to head the sales team in her company's new branch, and thanks to her newfound attitude, she was a shoo-in for the role. That's why I love sharing the gospel about adopting a buzzword.

I couldn't help but feel proud of Maya as she discovered how a simple shift in language had unlocked a world of possibilities and transformed her into someone who welcomed change with open arms.

"Taking breaks from gadgets and screens allows us to disconnect from the constant stream of information and engage more deeply with our thoughts and emotions.,." – Peter Bradford

**Start the Day on a Great Note:**

How we start our day can set the tone for the following hours. When Trendy Tactics expanded, I found it much easier to get through the tedious interviews and meetings when I had a great morning. First, I created a regular sleep pattern that helped me feel refreshed when I got out of bed in the morning. I read about a study published by the Proceedings of the National Academy of Science, which found that exposure to blue light the hour before bedtime led to delayed and disrupted sleep onset. So, I did away with my gadgets and focused on monitoring breathing patterns before dozing off.

Building a habit of sleeping well the previous night would kick start my day on a great note. When I combined that with physical activity like walking my dog and getting a delicious cup of coffee, I would be ready to take on whatever the company needed that day.

Creating a soundtrack of uplifting music also helped me get in the mindset to solve problems rather than complain. What you listen to has a way of affecting your energy for the rest of the day. So plug into whatever gives you energy, whether it's a podcast, affirmations, or your favorite artist rapping about being a boss.

Starting the day on the right foot and with the right attitude makes it easier to feel great throughout the day. Focus on something exciting that puts you in a great mood. Incorporating positive morning rituals, such as gratitude journaling, affirmations, or meditation, can give you the head start to bring your best and scale through changes.

## Meet Other "Great" People

During times of change, connecting with others who share our positive mindset can provide invaluable support. According to the Journal of Health and Social Behavior, people with strong social networks tend to have higher levels of psychological resilience and better emotional well-being. Surrounding ourselves with individuals who uplift and inspire us makes it easier to embrace change.

Think about it, knowing you've got people you can count on in times of need makes changes less daunting. It's a lot easier to go through life when you can go, "Damn, school is stressful right now, but I have awesome friends that make it interesting," or it can also be at work,

"My boss is really giving me a hard time, but I can always look forward to my husband making me laugh when I get home." On the other hand, surrounding yourself with people who deplete you can have the opposite effect. So, it's not enough to pull people who shine a light closer; you also must be intentional about keeping people who dim your light out.

With that said, understanding when your relationships are toxic is essential. If you have friends or family that constantly belittle your goals, erode your self-esteem, or drag you down with constant complaining, it might be time to set strict boundaries or walk away. I understand how difficult such a decision can be, especially when they're family.

Years before my mother passed, we'd had a complicated relationship. I loved her but didn't like her constantly calling me to complain about life. I would listen to her out of respect, but her words weighed down on me long after our conversation ended, and it took a toll on my mental health.

Knowing that it was draining my ability to be "great" and remain positive, I knew we had to have a difficult conversation. I explained to my mother how her constant negativity impacted me and flipped the tables by clarifying that she shouldn't call me if she had nothing nice to say.

I felt terrible for "cutting off" my mother, but I knew it was necessary to keep my circle positive. Luckily, she came around once she'd adopted a better mindset and even thanked me for helping her break the habit of talking negatively. Like me, she'd discovered how changing from a perspective of "good" to "excellent" can help you get through life with more ease and enthusiasm.

Surrounding yourself with positive and supportive people is crucial for your growth and happiness, as the people closest to you can be vital in helping you navigate life's transitions. I'm always eager to tell my friends and family how adopting a buzzword can transform their lives.

It's a lot easier to put the principles of this book into practice if the people around you understand and believe it, too. You need to take accountability for your circle if you want to be great.

## The Unwavering Power of Positivity

In a world where the only constant is change itself, the unwavering power of positivity shines as a beacon of hope. Despite receiving a grim prognosis, Stephen Hawkings chose to remain positive in the face of a progressively worsening condition to achieve his goals. When my ex-wife and I clashed following our divorce and evolving dynamics, I knew I had to reign over my negativity and remain civil to protect my daughter. Embracing change with a positive mindset allows us to thrive amidst uncertainty, making it easier to transform our lives from "good" to "excellent."

From envisioning a brighter future to prioritizing self-care, balancing your screen time, and checking your language, these simple shifts can reframe our experiences and motivate us as we embark on the journey of change. Priming your environment by starting your day on a great note, keeping a circle of like-minded people, and practicing positivity can also empower you to confront challenges whenever they arise. By nurturing a positive perspective, we can generate the much-needed momentum to propel us toward a life of greatness when people and situations change.

Chapter 8

**Changing One Word to BeeBetter**

After a few years in ATC doing sales, I realized it was time for another change, developing and executing fresh ideas to help the company grow had been exhilarating, but so I learned that I no longer liked the oppressive environment of a corporate company.

Sure, it provided stability, an asset everyone should aspire to. But it was simply "good enough" when I wanted great. My work in sales piqued my interest in business development over the years, and I fantasized about being a serial entrepreneur. I dreamed of starting a profitable business and empowering others to do the same. At this point, I'd stayed at ATC long enough to own shares that had risen exponentially as the company grew.

I did some mental calculations on their worth and realized that if I cashed out at the right time, I could earn almost half a million dollars. At the time, it was more money than I'd ever made, and my friend Kyle, who migrated to the US, joked about wishing he'd stay back so he could've had the same stock options. With that security blanket in mind, I decided to take a leap and pursue my budding passion.

The life of a serial entrepreneur was exciting. Between 1996 and 2009, I started at least four businesses. The "Talk 2" had started with so much promise, but my partner had screwed me by selling the process, and I had to make peace with it.

I moved on to selling domains and experimented with email lead generation, but I moved on when Facebook came on the scene. Sure, it'd been challenging starting and scaling multiple businesses. But I never felt like I was selling myself short or stagnant in my growth. It felt like I was on cloud 9, and with no significant roadblocks on the journey, embracing a "great" mindset was a breeze.

Eventually, I returned to my roots and started a software company. I wanted to focus on where my expertise lay: sales, so I brought in partners to manage operations and accounts. It was a great partnership. My new startup, Data Consort Tech, practically grew overnight, and I was impressed with how much my experience had helped. However, soon enough, I started to feel the pressure of what scaling up rapidly meant for me.

With the Data Consort growing, I had to bring in enough sales to cover operating costs, including the salaries of my partners. The pressure of knowing that it could mean not having food on the table for my partners was overwhelming if I didn't deliver. I spent countless hours devising new ways to drive sales; I could barely rest. I couldn't cut myself some slack. I couldn't sleep, knowing that if I had a bad month, other people and their families would suffer the consequences. It was suddenly a lot harder to be *great* with the mounting pressure.

I carried the crushing burden for two years before I could rekindle the circle of positivity that led me to think outside the box. With the Data Consort growing, I floated the idea of a sale to a competitor who happily absolved us into their camp.

In an ironic twist of fate, I craved the stability a bigger company provided, and I was more at ease knowing my partners, and I had a better safety blanket. Of course, the difference between when I'd left ATC and when I'd agreed to sell my software company was all the experience I had. And I'm not referring only to my resume.

"So, I learned that I no longer liked the oppressive environment of a corporate company." – Peter Bradford

My serial entrepreneurship journey helped me discover it's not always easy to be "great." You can easily falter when your partner betrays you or you're under a lot of stress. Without a detailed roadmap, you'll struggle to truly embrace the "great" mindset as life's struggles attempt to pull you underwater. Your degree of greatness might fluctuate depending on the circumstances, but it's essential to always live with it in mind, and here's how you can do it.

## Self-Reflection

A "great" mindset is characterized by ambition, passion, and a commitment to excellence. When I first spoke with Jean, he asked, "What will it take to be great?" Since that day, I've lived by those six words he uttered. Saying "I'm fine" or "I'm good" will have you settling for mediocrity regarding your goals. When I began to channel a "great" mindset, it spurred me to leave the comforts of "good" and go after my full potential.

It allowed me to transition to sales and then leap into business development. Transitioning from "good" to "great" begins with introspection. Ask yourself what areas of your life would benefit from an upgrade in your mindset. Taking time to assess where you've settled for what it would take to be "great" is the perfect place to start your journey to a new attitude.

## Setting Clear Goals

To shift to "great," you must set clear, specific, and inspiring goals. When I became a serial entrepreneur, I would set a goal to scale up till I was making a certain amount per month. With that figure in mind, I would devise actionable steps to get more leads, cut expenses, or bring in partners that could help me get there. Instead of vague notions of improvement, outline actionable steps that align with your vision of greatness. Define what "great" looks like for you in different areas of your life – career, relationships, personal growth – and establish a roadmap to get there.

Maybe you're an aspiring artist with a passion for painting; set a goal to exhibit at your local art gallery and then at a state gallery, and someday have your exhibition. Remember that setting clear, achievable goals will make it easier to commit and stay on track to be "great."

## Upgrading Language

A quote that goes, "You have two ears and one mouth; use them proportionately." Beyond making you a better listener, what you say goes a long way. Language and mindset are inseparable companions on the journey of personal growth. Our words reflect our thoughts, and our thoughts shape our reality.

Think about how you've casually replied with a "good" when asked how you're doing. It's time to recognize that the words we choose hold immense power.

When we adopt a "great" mindset, our language naturally follows suit, creating a cycle of positivity that affects our actions and interactions. When I say, "I feel," I get a surge of energy and enthusiasm for whatever I'm doing, and whoever I'm talking to instantly feels it.

It becomes a contagious and powerful expression that reframes how I act and how people react to me. Like when you smile at someone, and they smile back, using more positive words can cause an instant ripple effect. Language is the vehicle through which your mindset is conveyed to the world. So trade in your "fine" for "fantastic," your "okay" for "outstanding, "and "not bad" for "excellent.

Here's a comparison word bank to help you consciously align your speech with your improving and gradually getting "better" mindset.

| Say It | Trash It | Say It | Trash It |
|---|---|---|---|
| Amazing | ~~Tiring~~ | Interesting | ~~Annoying~~ |
| Brave | ~~Weak~~ | Terrific | ~~Terrible~~ |
| Gorgeous | ~~Overweight~~ | Hilarious | ~~Unnerving~~ |
| Funny | ~~Sad~~ | Exciting | ~~Dull~~ |
| Peachy | ~~Blue~~ | Golden | ~~Lost~~ |
| Winner | ~~Loser~~ | Strong | ~~Tired~~ |

**Taking Consistent Action**

A "great" mindset without action remains a mere intention. When I decided to grow out of the habit of saying "good," it was tough. I would yell it out as my reply whenever someone inquired, "How are you?" and kick myself for not remembering I was actually "great." Instead of giving up because I was too old to learn a new trick, I stuck with it. Even small actions accumulate over time, propelling you toward greatness, and soon, I was going to start switching careers, giving Academy-Award-worthy speeches, and starting my own business. Consistent action is the bridge between the ordinary and the extraordinary.

## Overcoming Challenges

Challenges are part of the journey to greatness. My career's most significant learning points have come from moments of deep uncertainty, confusion, and even mistakes. Rather than avoiding them, embrace them as opportunities for growth. When facing obstacles, remind yourself of your "great" mindset and determination to overcome.

Overcoming challenges is also easier when you develop strategies for navigating the storm through problem-solving or seeking support. I like to face obstacles head-on, so it immediately resonated with me when I stumbled on the 5-second rule.

The 5-second rule is a powerful metacognition technique that overrides the brain's tendency to squash your good ideas and intentions. It was discovered by Mel Robbins when her life was spiraling downwards. It's an interesting solution to help you break the habit loop and start acting on things you have meant to do for years. Ironically, Mel stumbled on this hack at one of the lowest points in her life.

Through a series of unfortunate events, Mel wasn't working. Her husband owned a pizza restaurant and had to work exceptionally long hours to keep the business afloat, and money was always hard to come by.

Thanks to their financial situation, Mel had developed a habit of drinking in the evenings, and her confidence and self-esteem were at an all-time low. Unfortunately, feeling bad about her life meant Mel didn't want to face the day when morning came.

When the alarm clock went off, she felt dread and would press the snooze button until she could no longer ignore it, and her mornings would be frantic as she tried to pack homework and lunch before missing the school bus.

Mel felt she was failing her kids, creating a cycle of negativity. Every night, she would say, 'Tomorrow, I will get up on the first ring of the alarm.' She knew her whole day would be significantly better if she could do that. Yet, no matter how good her intentions were at nighttime, she would press snooze again in the morning.

Then, one evening, as Mel was on her way to bed, the TV caught her attention, and she saw a rocket launched into space. She heard the countdown. 5-4-3-2-1 launch!

"That is it!" she thought, "When the alarm rings tomorrow, I will say 5-4-3-2-1 and launch myself out of bed."

It worked! And the next day… and the next after that…

Mel couldn't quite believe that something so simple was helping. She would even use the 5-second rule to curb her impulsivity. She'd count down and walk away whenever Mel poured one too many drinks. If she were arguing with her spouse, in 5-4-3-2-1, she would apologize or adjust her tone.

Her husband noticed the positive changes and asked her what she was doing differently. He tried the 5 Second Rule, and it worked for him too. Then their friends started to use it, and they also found it powerful.

When Mel did a TEDx talk, she mentioned the 5-second solution towards the end of her speech, which went viral. After receiving so many tweets and emails with victory stories, Mel researched why it was effective.

She discovered that when someone has an idea to do something, whether as big as starting a business or as small as getting off the sofa, there is always a moment of hesitation. At that moment, your brain tries to talk you out of it; it comes up with problems or reasons not to act: 'Most businesses fail, that is a lot of work,' or 'It's very comfortable here,' making you feel defeated and recline to your comfort zone.

However, when you have an idea or intention and start counting backward from 5 to 1, your brain can not talk you out of it because you are counting. Even your clever brain can only do one thing at a time.

Then, because you start to move physically, the prefrontal cortex is activated, and rather than slipping into default mode, which would keep you repeating old patterns like hitting the snooze button, it supports you as you create new ones. By happy accident, Mel discovered a powerful metacognition technique that breaks the 'habit loop.'

Overthinking, procrastination, indecision, self-doubt, worry, and perfectionism can make it harder to get out of your way when facing an obstacle. When you face challenges that overwhelm you, it can feel frustrating knowing you have the ability, but acting feels out of reach. These scenarios are where the 5 Second Rule comes in. It bridges the gap and gets you out of your head so that you can start taking helpful actions.

Whatever strategies you adopt to overcome challenges, take small steps today. Remember that challenges are growth opportunities, and you can use them as a stepping stone to a greater life.

Mel couldn't quite believe that something so simple was helping. She would even use the 5-second rule to curb her impulsivity. She'd count down and walk away whenever Mel poured one too many drinks. If she were arguing with her spouse, in 5-4-3-2-1, she would apologize or adjust her tone.

Her husband noticed the positive changes and asked her what she was doing differently. He tried the 5 Second Rule, and it worked for him too. Then their friends started to use it, and they also found it powerful.

Mel discovered a powerful metacognition technique that breaks the 'habit loop.' Overthinking, procrastination, indecision, self-doubt, worry, and perfectionism can make it harder to get out of your way when facing an obstacle. When you face challenges that overwhelm you, it can feel frustrating knowing you have the ability, but acting feels out of reach.

These scenarios are where the 5 Second Rule comes in. It bridges the gap and gets you out of your head so that you can start taking helpful actions. Whatever strategies you adopt to overcome challenges, take small steps today. Remember that challenges are growth opportunities; you can use them as a stepping stone to a more excellent life.

## Cultivating Resilience

Resilience is the cornerstone of maintaining a "great" mindset. It's the ability to bounce back from setbacks, adapt to change, and keep moving forward. A quote by Timber Hawkeye goes,

*"You can't calm the storm, so stop trying. What you can do is calm yourself. The storm will pass."*

Of course, calming your mind is easier said than done. In the past, Lynette struggled with keeping her mind from racing, even in the most calming circumstances. From a rock about ten feet tall near her house, she would watch as the sunset and the lights of thousands of houses began to flicker like fireflies. She'd feel the cold wind on her face and listen to the dogs' bark, teenagers laugh, and the low hum of traffic.

Despite the picture scene, she would fixate on the intense ball of worry that felt like crushing her chest, a manifestation of the physical tension from restlessly attempting to solve new problems. Her life was relentless anxiety. For years, Lynette didn't understand why she would get so anxious and couldn't relax either.

"Was I just born with a sensitive nervous system? Had life experiences conditioned me to be that way?" She would ask. Ultimately, it didn't matter. Anxiety was there, making itself heard, loud and clear.

Fortunately, by embracing a "great" mindset, Lynette began to practice calming her body and mind. However, she learned that her anxiety could be tamed and reversed. But it was after she'd brought greater awareness to her body and progressively convinced her nervous system that she was safe that any lasting change could occur.

If you have a susceptible jumpy system, here are some ways to calm it:

**Focus on the calmest part of your body.**

Instead of sitting directly with uncomfortable feelings, sensations, and tensions, place your attention wherever you find a sense of calm in your body. Doing that lets you familiarize yourself with relaxation and sit with it until it deepens. For example, your legs may be twitching, but perhaps you feel stillness at the back of your neck. Draw your attention there.

**Set boundaries and manage your energy wisely.**

If you're dealing with anxiety, you burn more energy than usual. And when your point is low, it's more challenging to regulate your feelings. That's why it's essential to manage your power wisely, not be afraid to set boundaries and say no to things you don't feel are in your best interest.

**Self-soothe through affirmations.**

Affirmations are only valid if they're having a helpful impact on your state of being. Repeating positive phrases you don't honestly believe in can have the opposite effect. So, instead, choose an affirmation that feels true to you, such as "I am strong enough to survive this panic." Try experimenting with how you talk to yourself—the tone of voice, pace, and care behind the words—instead of just the words you are saying. A slow, calm, and reassuring internal voice can be a great tool to calm the body.

**Journal from the perspective of your stress.**

Sometimes, your anxious thoughts must be respected and expressed coherently by getting them out of your head and down on paper. Writing from the perspective of stress, exploring what's fueling it and what it wants us to know, also helps us take a step back from our worries.

**Journal from the perspective of your calm.**

When you've written down your stressful thoughts, you can dialogue (and reason) with them from the perspective of a calmer and wiser voice.

**Try Taoist Inner Smile Meditation.**

This meditation is one where you feel a smiling energy in your body. Most people find this easiest to do by visualizing a smile or bringing a slight smile to their faces. The effect of the inner smile meditation is cumulative, and it can effectively signal to your brain that you're not under any threat. Finish the sentence "My nervous system wants to…" This journal exercise helps connect your thoughts to your feelings so you can take a step back from your thoughts.

You may discover that your nervous system wants you to take a break, rest, or get some fresh air.

**Create compassionate imagery.**

Like the inner smile meditation, compassionate imagery is a way to tell your brain that you're safe and it's okay to relax. You should visualize a person or a place, real or fictitious, where you'd feel the most calm, secure, and connected.

**Increase bodily awareness.**

Anxiety can feel like it comes out of nowhere, but that's rarely true. By increasing bodily awareness through meditation, yoga, or regularly checking in with how you're feeling, you can catch the early signs of tension in your body before they get too difficult to manage.

**Slow down to six breaths a minute.**

Studies have shown that six breaths a minute is the number at which we get the most benefits in terms of relaxation. That's one breath every ten seconds. As most of us breathe a lot quicker than this, any attempt to reduce our breathing rate—by focusing on extending the exhalation—is a valuable practice. Breathe in through your nose for five seconds, breathe out through your mouth for another five, and bam: magic, six breaths a minute.

**Play around with your body language.**

How we position our bodies and physically move through the world dramatically impacts our emotional state. Bringing more awareness to how you're holding your body from moment to moment—how you sit, stand, communicate, etc.—can help you address habits of tension.

**Establish a mindful movement practice.**

Remembering to be aware of our bodies can be tricky, which is why a daily or weekly embodiment practice is beneficial. Try yoga, qigong tai chi, the Feldenkrais method, the Alexander Technique, or any other exercise. Just try to find something you enjoy, and that works for you.

**Dance.**

Dancing is a great way to reduce stress and increase your bodily awareness. Dance might be for you if you prefer something other than a formal practice. And the good thing is you don't need to get any special training or even leave your house—you can blast your favorite song and get moving.

**Visualize a future calm self.**

Our minds are largely predictive machines, so when we expect to be anxious, that's what will happen. We can begin to disrupt this cycle by visualizing a future state of calm, which sets a more useful expectation.

**Imagine your mind in slow motion.**

This is just another trick to break out of unhelpful patterns. An anxious mind will rush, whereas a mind that is intentionally moving slowly will start to move us out of a state of anxiety.

**Laugh (even if it's forced).**

Laughter is another excellent way to take our body out of a state of stress. The reason we laugh might be an evolutionary signal that everything is okay and that a perceived threat has been averted. It doesn't matter if it feels forced; your brain will still get the message, and you might even find that you laugh anyway.

**Try chanting or singing meditation.**

Both chanting and singing slow your breathing down and stimulate the vague nerve, which is another quick way to transition from a fight-or-flight state to rest and digest. Some people don't like to chant or sing, but luckily, humming does pretty much the same thing.

**Visualize healthy and rewarding social situations.**

A lot of bodily tension comes from an unconscious perceived threat in the world—particularly the social world. By visualizing healthy relationships and positive social situations, real or imagined, we are convincing the social part of our brain that we're connected and safe. There is no best way to manage our nervous systems. There is only one way that works for you. By permitting yourself to experiment and play around with different techniques, you'll be better able to cultivate resilience and overcome adversity.

## Celebrating Progress

As you progress towards greatness, take moments to celebrate your progress. Whenever my businesses crossed a certain monetary threshold, I always took time out to celebrate with my team. It didn't matter if it was the first or fifth business; each milestone was worth the hype.

# Living the "Great" Life

I was at ease after selling Data Tech Corp to another software company. In exchange for all the hard work my partners and I had put in, we got stocks and a guaranteed monthly salary for the next two years at least! It was one of my proudest moments; I felt fulfilled thinking about all the experiences that had led up to that moment. My journey hadn't been without its challenges. I'd doubted myself initially, made mistakes that would eat at me for years, and parted unfriendly with some business partners. But with my inner mantra and outward expression of the phrase, "I'm great," each step propelled me toward my goal.

Remember, the journey to greatness is ongoing. You need to reflect on where you're "good" and set clear goals to be more. Transitioning from "good" to "great" is not just a linguistic shift; it's a transformation of your entire being. By deliberating and embracing a "great" mindset, you're stepping into a life of fulfillment, success, and positive impact, and every day presents an opportunity to choose "great" over "good." And when you start to harness the results, always celebrate your progress. Please share your experiences, insights, and successes with others, encouraging them to embark on their paths to greatness.

## Chapter 9

### Life is a Journey, not a Destination

I'm grateful that my parents instilled in me the love of exploration and the joy of shared experiences when I was young. Planting the desire for the open road was one thing they did well that would spark my love for travel. Sure, we had material things that made life much more convenient, but our road trips made me see the value of prioritizing different experiences.

Beach resorts or luxury hotels weren't staples of our summers. My dad wasn't a fan of flying, so we drove everywhere we could. Packed in a C-class motorhome, we would revel in the hum of the highway, the unknown adventures waiting for us, and the magic of togetherness.

It was important to my parents that we see as much of the country as possible, so the summer we got the motorhome, we embarked on a journey across the vast expense of Canada. I remember how excited I was as we loaded up, ready to venture into the unknown. My sister and I spent most of our time in the upper layer watching our black-and-white TV with its rabbit ear antennas, waiting for the next stop.

During our journey, we met so many friendly people in different provinces. It was thrilling to see how diverse and exciting our country is. On our first trip, we drove through the West Coast, visiting some famous landmarks in British Columbia and participating in the Calgary Stampede.

When we hit the East Coast the following year, I was in awe when we saw Anne of Green Gables on Prince Edward Island and took a ferry to Newfoundland. I formed truly unforgettable memories from our visits, but the best part was the time we spent together.

Cooped up with my parents and sister for long drives for multiple days created a special bond between us. The resounding sound of laughter, the shared meals in cozy campgrounds, and the discovery of the world we lived in. It opened my eyes to how people lived and how strangers could be warm and inviting. Of course, being stuck in the motorhome with my family for so long wasn't always a bed of roses. As you can imagine, we stepped on each other's toes quite a b it.

My sister and I would bicker often, but we had to learn to settle our differences and find a way to get along for the ride. I quickly learned the importance of staying flexible and rolling with problems when they came along.

These trips weren't just about going places; they were mini lessons in teamwork and understanding. Looking back, I know that these encounters shaped me and catalyzed my ability to adapt, socialize, and learn early on that life's most significant treasures are often found in the journey itself.

Wisely, Ralph Waldo Emerson once said that life is indeed a journey, not a destination, and examining my past, I can't help but agree with him. When I think about my life, the experiences with my loved ones shine the brightest, and I'm sure it's the same for you.

In hindsight, some of the silly arguments and travel mishaps were amusing memories.

You probably have personal stories where things didn't go as planned or of a dear friend who might have started out as a rival. While it's not always easy to overcome failure or opposition, using them as a stepping stone can make those adversities worth it when we look back on our lives.

As I grew older, I felt motivated by my experiences to be a better parent. With so many memories and lessons learned from my time on the road, I want Emma to have the same. I wanted her to learn to relish in the moments without the thought of the destination consuming the present. I want everybody to see that the smiles, tears, laughs, fights, pitstops, and endless drives are all the building blocks of a great life.

## The Power of Learning from Struggles

Looking back on my life, it might have been tempting to throw in the towel years ago if I had known even half of the struggles I would encounter.

The self-doubt as I watched my friend scale the corporate ladder while I wondered if I was making the right choice. The pain of watching my marriage crumble and coming to terms with the fact the family I'd once desired would have to take a different shape, and the turbulence of being a serial entrepreneur that often came with seeing the worst sides of people. Yet, those trials and tribulations forced me to adapt, encouraged me to evolve, and ultimately showed me the strength and power I had within me.

Throughout life, we are bound to encounter obstacles and setbacks. However, it's crucial to understand that these challenges are not roadblocks. On the contrary, they are the perfect tools to create an incredible life with the satisfaction of knowing we weathered the storm. I've learned that fulfillment comes from knowing you've learned from the complex and painful lessons you've endured.

Think about how satisfying it feels when you finally solve a puzzle or watch the hero scale through impossible odds. When you talk about your greatest achievement, I'm confident it comes with a backstory to what obstacles or challenges you had to face to get there. The truth is triumph is incomplete without struggle, and the sooner we learn to accept that it all serves a purpose on a far grander scale than we can currently comprehend, the better and happier we'll be.

So, I encourage you to consider whatever roadblocks you're facing with positivity, knowing that one day you'll look back and say - "Why, of course, I didn't see it at the time, but that had to happen to allow room for that opportunity" or "Who would've guessed my mistakes would prepare me for the next chapter in my life?"

When I first heard the lyrics to American musician Andy Grammar's song, 'I wish you pain,' I was startled. I was sure it was a song wishing your worst enemy the most gut-wrenching feelings of worthlessness, physical burden, and loneliness. And with wishes for doubts, insight terror like monsters, and people breaking their promises, leaving the person the song is directed to in the cold, could you blame me? So, imagine my amazement when I discovered the artist dedicated the song to his daughter.

After painting a vivid picture of all the terrible things Andy wishes for, the song's hook and chorus reveal that although it's hard to want these things for your loved one, it's important because the heart only grows when it breaks. As a parent whose first instinct is to protect and provide the best for my child, it seems counterintuitive to resonate with Andy Grammar's song. Nobody wants to go through painful experiences; we all want our lives to be easy. But life never grants us that wish. Instead, it forces us to put our mettle to the test. So, despite its unconventional message of, "I love you, so I wish you pain," it's crucial to recognize that struggles force us to tap into our inner strength, fostering resilience and grit that might otherwise remain untapped.

## Early Struggles

For many of us, lessons from struggle begin early, even in the classroom. I've never been a fan of the traditional school system. I've realized that not every kid learns the same, yet we force everyone to absorb and regurgitate content the same way. I'll always advocate for making our schooling system more engaging and memorable. As a child, I was never a big reader, and while I didn't struggle in school, I wasn't motivated to learn more than I had to. One of the biggest reasons for my indifference toward reading is that I typically forgot most of what I read. Pouring over the boring texts in my schoolbooks, I would quickly find myself tuning out, leaving me with no recollection of what I'd just read. Of course, because it was required to pass, I would have to go over it again, missing key points along the way and continuing a vicious cycle.

As I got older, I discovered I was more attuned to listening than reading physical texts. I developed a love for audiobooks and found that it was easier for me to retain information. Learning became more exciting when I could hear a voiceover vividly detailing the scenarios and explaining the material I needed to learn.

Although I didn't abandon written books altogether, I discovered I was less likely to space out when the author used relevant stories. Take any textbook and convert it to stories that teach the same content; I guarantee that kids will easily absorb what you're trying to teach. Interactive stories will make them more excited to learn, and they will also make them stick to their memories. So, it'll be easier to recall relevant information during exams by remembering a story they heard in class. At the end of the day, stories do more than make learning materials more engaging; they connect with us on an emotional level that trumps the traditional structure most of us are familiar with.

Yet, despite its shortcomings, there are people whose stories are a testament to the power of turning struggle into strengths. Successful Olympian Michael Phelps is one such example. It might've been hard to picture young Michael growing up to earn 28 Olympic medals for his prowess in swimming. He found it incredibly difficult to sit still in school and focus on his studies, a far cry from the dedication required to become an athlete.

Realizing that his restlessness and lack of focus were abnormal, Michael was diagnosed with ADHD at age 6. Still, despite his learning restriction, his teachers continuously insisted he calm down and pay attention, making no adjustments for him to learn better. Naturally, since he struggled with completing assignments and staying on track with his responsibilities, it didn't seem like he had a 'great' future ahead of him.

Concerned about her son's growing struggle, Michael's mother decided to take matters into her own hands. If the school and its teachers weren't equipped to provide a supportive learning environment for her child, she would have to do it herself. Michael had always had an affinity for water, and it struck Mrs. Phelps that swimming could be an excellent avenue for him to channel his excess energy and regain more focus in class. Unknown to her, she'd set her son on a trajectory that would change his life.

Swimming had started out as the ideal outlet for Michael to use up all his energy constructively. A space where his hyperactivity would be an asset rather than a liability, and it was. He quickly fell in love with the sport and would spend hours in the water working on his technique and speed. Michael's ADHD-driven hyper-focus became a crucial ingredient to his success story. Although he'd struggled with paying attention in other areas of his life, swimming was different. The pool was his sanctuary, and all his focus was on being the best.

By age 10, Michael's effort began to pay off significantly. He created a new national record for his age group in the 100-meter butterfly race and went on to clinch several records as he grew. His prowess in the water would connect him with Bob Bowman, a renowned swim coach who quickly recognized his talent and resilience.

Together, they could channel what had once been a weakness into an advantage that set Michael Phelps apart from his competitors. In the beginning, his ADHD had been a pesky obstacle to thriving in the traditional education setting society had placed on him. However, Michael found a way to turn his weakness into a strength that made him triumphant. With the proper support, a strong sense of purpose, and a determination to leverage his unique qualities, he turned an uphill battle into a slide to victory.

Whether you're struggling with the current educational system or a society forcing you to conform unnaturally, remember that it can still be an opportunity for growth. With some creativity, a stumbling block can become a stepping stone, and your obstacles can become a launchpad in your journey to success.

## Nurturing Relationships and Experiences

Life and its struggles are inseparable pieces of the same puzzle. And while we can use positivity to see our roadblocks as a path to success, it helps when you're not alone. Triumph isn't limited solely to our achievements; it extends to our relationships and shared experiences. Our interactions with loved ones and the memories we create together make our journey through life more enjoyable. Unfortunately, I didn't always understand this, and reflecting on my past, I can remember times I could've been kinder to the people I loved.

While summers were for road trips and living on the road, my childhood winters were more laid back. I spent many weekends with my grandparents and hanging out with my friends. One of my favorite activities was going snowmobiling. It was exhilarating to have the white snow whip around as my friends and I cruised as fast as we could.

Leading up to my winter in the sixth grade, I'd had to save money from my allowance to replace the windshield of my snowmobile. It was a lot of work earning and putting aside $100 at the time, but I eagerly stacked my piggy bank till I could afford a replacement.

After getting a brand-new windshield, I was pleased and looked forward to spending winter break with a snow trail behind me. But life had other plans for me. I vividly remember seeing my sister walking down the lane with tears streaming down her face as she said, "Peter," with a shaky breath. I knew instantly something was wrong. She'd taken my snowmobile out for a ride and walked back home on foot.

"*Where's my snowmobile?*" I screamed at her instantly.

"I ran into a tree. I'm sorry." She'd explained, obviously still distraught.

Naturally, when a loved one is in an accident, your first concern should be their safety. But as a child, I was much more self-centered and pissed that she'd broken my brand-new windscreen, even though it wasn't intentional.

Thankfully, my sister wasn't hurt, and the broken windscreen left no lasting scars between us. We still showed up for each other when it mattered the most, our achievements and failures becoming a reason to celebrate together or lean on each other.

In hindsight, that unfortunate event that felt like the end of the world to me is now a funny story we can retell at family gatherings. Such a seemingly minor incident now echoes the decades of history between us and strengthens our bond.

So, when I had my daughter, I knew I wanted to have similar experiences with her. When Emma was three years old, in a bid to recreate my childhood, I went out and bought us snowmobiles. Emma was excited when she saw the snowmobiles and would call the two-stroke machine "super speed." It was such a thrilling experience seeing something that had brought me joy as a child do the same for my daughter. Most days, Emma would anxiously wait till evenings so we could go on another trip.

She gleefully squealed and laughed as we made it down the snow-covered slopes, with no concerns other than avoiding the obstacles in front of her. And after hours of riding, she would fall asleep soundly, content with how the day had gone.

Watching her go to sleep after being part of such an enjoyable day would always put me in a great mood, regardless of what was happening at work. It always did. Going on road trips, trying new activities, or simply spending quality time with my family created memories that outweighed my individual successes and failures—those moments of human connection reminded me that life is a shared journey. It's not a lonely road or a rickety bridge you have to pass one at a time. It's a voyage where you're the captain, and the people you bring along with you are your crew.

So carving out time to be there and nurture those relationships makes your ship strong enough to sail through open waters and survive the harshest storms. Looking back at my childhood, I'm grateful that the adventurous trips with my parents made it easier to see the value in togetherness and unity.

As I navigated the heartbreaking distance my divorce put between myself and my daughter Emma, I knew it was necessary to create the kind of memories with her that my parents did with me. So, I made a deliberate effort to foster our communication, speaking with her on the phone every day and visiting (or having her visit me) at every opportunity.

Family is the most important thing in the world, and I can't emphasize that too much. In the book, "The Top Five Regrets of the Dying," palliative care nurse Bronnie Ware recorded that one of the most common regrets people have towards the end of their life is not spending enough time with family and friends. It's not having more money in their bank account or spending more hours at the office.

Multiple studies also support Bronnie's research, showing the significance of spending quality time with your family and loved ones so you don't live a life of regret at the end of it. I'm not ignorant that I was lucky growing up, either. Not everyone can boast about having a family that was as tightly bonded as mine then or now.

But no matter where you're at with your loved ones, I strongly encourage you to be intentional about working on yourself and working on your relationships. Whether it's the family you make or the one you're born into, forming deep connections that matter can be a powerful source of inspiration to overcome challenges and reach new heights.

## Cultivating Genuine Bonds

While I tried my best to replicate my childhood for my daughter with snowmobiles and road trips, I was aware that she may not have taken well to all the things I enjoyed. Sure, it's fantastic when the people you love share the same likes as you. Having the same aspirations and values can be a vital source of motivation and encouragement.

However, avoiding falling into the trap of wanting to foster connections based solely on what you want, or need is essential. That doesn't make for a supportive ecosystem and can be counterintuitive. Many people might say, "I hope my kid grows up to be like me," and I don't necessarily agree with that. I don't want Emma to be exactly like me. I want her to take from the best parts of me and build on them. We have a tradition where we go out for breakfast every Sunday to talk and check in with each other.

It would be awesome if that's a tradition she'd like to continue with her kids. But I'd rather she does something more specific to her children's needs in a way that immortalizes her in their memory as a fantastic parent. In a world filled with superficial connections, genuine relationships are a triumph. And genuine bonds are only possible when others are free to be themselves.

So, encourage your loved ones to try new things with you, but remember to strike a balance between being in a safe place and pushing them forward. In the end, you'll find that cultivating genuine bonds with supportive individuals who uplift and inspire you can help to transcend from the boundaries of *sound* to the pinnacle of *greatness*.

## The Happiness of Pursuing Passion

At the heart of the journey from good to great is the pursuit of one's passion. The true definition of passion is fulfilling our life's purpose. And I don't necessarily mean in a spiritual sense; I mean that our purpose is to find happiness within ourselves, and we can only do that when what we do aligns with our deepest values. One of my deepest values has always been to help people. I embarked on this project in the first place: to show people how changing one word can transform their lives. Replacing good with great has shaped the trajectory of my entire life for the better, and at my core, I'm not the kind of person who can keep it to myself.

In the relationships I've intentionally nurtured, the story of how going from a 'good' to a 'great' mindset has helped me overcome struggle is well known. Another core value for me is freedom. After my conversation with Jean, I realized that 'great' for me wasn't being tied to a corporate job. It was the flexibility to grow, try new things, and start again when I failed. And while I understand that dream requires people ready to stay and build, it's why I've always prioritized giving my employees and partners the flexibility they need to work efficiently.

Knowing that I value flexibility and helping others, it's no wonder why I've always found myself attracted to jobs that help others grow.

Whether it's creating innovative sales solutions to boost performance or helping small businesses stand out and increase their brand's visibility. Finding different roles that meet the intersection of my values and interests has made me truly wealthy. And when I say wealth, I don't necessarily mean in terms of bank account balance; I'm referring to happiness. Even if I had a billion dollars, I would never retire. I would still wake up dedicated to doing what I do because that makes me feel great. Many people get caught up in a rat race where they'll be happy if they get that next thing. "When I buy my dream home, I'll be satisfied," "When I get promoted to VP, I'll be happy," "When I get married, I'll be at peace." But in those scenarios, achieving these, while monumental feats are incredible, creates a pattern where happiness is an ever-futuristic trophy they can't attain.

For anyone with a huge dream, an even bigger one appears when they achieve the objective. When we discover the true essence of triumph is in those little moments of genuine happiness and satisfaction with our lives, we can stop running in the rat race. Imagine a painter reveling in pride after spending multiple hours meticulously working on a canvas, a teacher seeing the "aha!" moment in her student's eyes, or a scientist developing a cure that helps millions. A cheque can never replicate such moments of authentic joy and rewarding fulfillment. Where our passions intertwine with purpose, happiness goes beyond monetary gains.

Pursuing passion enriches your life story, making your journey from good to excellent a true triumph.

## The Unending Triumph

My ongoing decision to go from being good to great constantly reminds me that life is a continuous journey. Over the years, it has become significantly easier for me to believe and say, "I'm great." Still, because I'm human, when adversities come along, it takes a second for me to remember to be optimistic despite the situation.

You will encounter successes and failures throughout your life, shaping your character and path. But it's crucial to remember that triumph is remaining positive in facing struggles, nurturing meaningful relationships, and pursuing your passions. To round off with Andy Grammar's unconventional message, I wish that your heart can grow and that you are triumphant despite life's inevitable pains.

Chapter 10

**Power of Transformation, Reflecting on the Journey**

In my forties, I realized something profound: I'd rather spend quality time with my daughter, Emma, than spend money on material things.

Not that those things were unimportant; I've always sought to give my daughter everything she needs. I simply realized they were less important than our shared experiences. After all, memories far outlive material possessions. That realization echoes the core of the BeeBetter Movement, where being positive and being great is not a matter of what you have but who you are. It's the commitment to always look on the brighter side of things and strive to be better every day, irrespective of what you own or are going through.

My decision to invest my time and energy in Emma instead of splurging on stuff wasn't extravagant, but it turned out to be one the best ones I've ever made. Of course, the foundation for my shift in priorities began long before I encountered Jean. I was lucky to have a family that prioritized life on the road and shared spaces over the latest gadgets.

And these lessons weren't limited to my childhood summers; I imbibed them from my extended family all year round. When I was a kid, my grandparents' home was a major highlight of our weekends. Fifty acres of vast woodland, complete with a pond, a main house, and an A-frame cabin on the pond's edge, made it the prime location for adventures in the woods. I was truly living every little boy's dream.

My grandfather and I were an inseparable duo during these weekend visits. He was my guide, mentor, and friend. It was through him I learned to appreciate the wonders of nature. I remember paying close attention with giddy excitement as he taught me about various bird species. And when we weren't considering different beaks, feathers, and talons, we tapped trees to collect sap and boil it down to syrup. The transformation was nothing short of magic to me, and I would excitedly load the liquid onto my tiny snow caboose, eager to take it home and show everyone else what we'd done. Our self-made maple syrup was like a sweet liquid golden trophy.

I loved the woods not only because it was a place of learning but because it was the perfect site for adventure. I would often invite my friends to join us on the grounds, and we spent our days building forts, complete with moats and drawbridges made from bits of wood. Then, after a long day of imaginary battle, we would camp under the starlit sky, enjoying the best parts of our childhood.

Beyond being nostalgic, I shared this story as a reminder of the beauty of simplicity. This story is a way to highlight the importance of bonding with your loved ones.

It is the concept at the heart of the BeeBetter movement - that one word can help us embrace our childlike manner of cherishing moments, nurturing connections, and growing through shared experiences.

As we embark on the final chapter of this journey, it's important to reminisce over what we've learned so far and how it all comes full circle to how one word can redefine our perspective on life and contribute to a better future. These final pages culminate the wisdom we've gathered along this journey, a testament to my belief that the power of personal transformation should not stay within these pages. We should share it with the world.

The BeeBetter Movement is a call to revolt and lay waste to your old selves. To let go of everything that holds you down. It's a call to use a single word, to rewrite your narrative, and to redefine your destiny. But it's not just about personal growth; it's also about spreading positivity and kindness to others. It's about rewriting the pages of our lives, one word at a time, and inspiring others to do the same.

## Purpose and Meaning

Negativity often clouds our job satisfaction; for many of you, complaining about your work may be the norm. However, the BeeBetter Movement encourages a different approach. It calls us to start every day with a burst of enthusiasm.

Consider the difference between saying, "I'm doing good today," versus "I'm doing great today!" While the first implies a static generic good enough state, the latter radiates energy and enthusiasm. It doesn't just report on your day; it's a manifestation of a positive outlook that can influence the course of your life.

When you consistently replace "good" with "great," you change more than your vocabulary. You transform your mindset to be more optimistic and open. And with this shift, you can align your newfound positivity with experiences that make you feel more authentic when you use your buzzword.

In an attempt to discover "what it would take to be great," you become more willing to take risks, explore new horizons, and seek opportunities that bring you closer to your true purpose.

When I discovered my buzzword, "I'm great," the first place I applied it was my job. It challenged me to shift from being "good" to truly embracing the idea of being "great" and drove me to pursue paths that unlocked my potential. Now, I'm challenging you to BeeAmazing at Work. Whether you're self-employed, working for a company, or an individual, the path to workplace greatness begins with a shift in perspective.

**Discovering Purpose Through Transformation**

Although I was never a Boy Scout, I often admire their core values of proper preparation and arming yourself with a plan. These attributes lay the foundation for success in the jungles of nature and life. To be amazing at your job, you must approach your work with pride, deriving fulfillment from every task you accomplish. Set goals and track your progress meticulously, constantly asking yourself how you can *beebetter*. These qualities are essential for individual growth and fostering your "flow state" at work.

A flow state is a zone of deep concentration where distractions melt away, and our minds are free to soar. Achieving this state brings us inner peace amid chaos and helps us break free from negative cycles in support of something new. When we can pause, reset, and change our reactions, we step closer to fulfillment in our everyday lives.

When you consistently choose "great" over "good," you pause, achieving this deep flow state, and begin to live your life with intention and purpose. You recognize that every day is an opportunity to contribute positively to the world and leave a lasting impact.

A quote by David Viscott goes, "The purpose of life is to discover your gift, and the meaning of life is to give it away," and I can't help but agree with the famed psychiatrist and author. Every one of us possesses a unique gift, a talent, an exceptional quality that defines us authentically. That's why The BeeBetter Movement emphasizes the importance of being mindful of our self-talk. Positive self-talk boosts self-esteem, improves moods, and motivates us to reach our goals. In contrast, negative self-talk leads to anxiety, depression, and diminished self-esteem.

Embracing encouraging self-talk and practicing gratitude creates a positive mindset that attracts positivity into our lives. By using the word, any of the buzzwords that you have selected for yourself, is a subtle daily reminder that you're on a mission to make use of your gifts, achieve your full potential, and live a life of purpose.

> "When I discovered my buzzword, "I'm great," the first place I applied it was my job." – Peter Bradford

## Our Words & Relationships

The impact of words cannot be overstated, especially in our relationships. Words can uplift, inspire, and encourage our loved ones. In contrast, they can also tear down, hurt, and destroy. The bonds we form are the essence of our existence, and the people we love can be our greatest motivation to do better. One of the most heartwarming stories Lynette has shared with me is about her personal growth as a parent by choosing to *BeeBetter*. As a dedicated mom, she often grapples with her children's constant chatter and endless questions. Earlier on, Lynette would struggle to balance her need to concentrate on work with answering their never-ending inquiries.

While she took pride in their curiosity, especially since they were homeschooled, there were times when Lynette needed silence. Instead of getting frustrated, Lynette chose understanding. She gathered her kids and gently spoke to them.

*"I love your questions,"* she said, *"but I can't listen all day. What if we have specific times when you talk, and I listen carefully?"*

The idea excited her kids, and they agreed. But Lynette took it a step further. She introduced a game to teach them a crucial life skill, and that's the ability to be silent. They set a timer and began with just one minute of quiet time. It was challenging, especially for the youngest, who couldn't resist making some noise. Yet, the older kids surprised everyone by staying completely silent. They calmly sat with Lynette, watching the timer, eagerly waiting for the next challenge.

Eventually, they progressed to 2, 3, and even 6 minutes of silence. Lynette understood that teaching her kids when to speak and when to be quiet was essential. It wasn't just for her own peace but also to equip them with crucial skills in dealing with the world around them. In a world where constant chatter can be disruptive and unkind, teaching them to be considerate of others was a valuable lesson.

This story of Lynette and her children shows how our actions and words can influence our relationships. Lynette's patient approach nurtured her children's understanding, empathy, and respect for others. Words are mighty in our relationships. They can uplift, inspire, and encourage our loved ones, or they can hurt and create distance.

Think about when someone's words made you feel like you could conquer the world or when another made you feel small and unimportant. These words can stick with us for a long time, shaping our self-esteem and relationships.

That's why realizing how much our words impact our loved ones is essential.

Choosing our words carefully and thoughtfully can make all the difference. Simple positives like "thank you," "I love you," and "I appreciate you" can be the building blocks of solid and healthy relationships. They convey value and care, reminding our loved ones of their importance. On the other hand, negative words like "you never," "you always," and "I don't care" can damage our relationships. They can make our loved ones feel unheard, undervalued, and unloved. So, words play a significant role in our relationships. They can either strengthen our bonds or weaken them. By consciously choosing positive comments and avoiding negative ones, we can build thriving, long-lasting relationships that enrich our lives and the lives of those we care about. By recognizing our interconnectedness, we can nurture relationships that help us succeed and see *greatness* where it was previously only good.

## Transformation and Growth

Since the first chapter of this book, we've embarked on a journey to see how the default 'good' can mean accepting mediocrity and how the pursuit of 'great' can transform your life for the better. I explained how your language affects what you visualize, and what you imagine spurs you to strive for more.

By understanding that words have immense power and shifting our mindset from 'good' to 'great,' we can alter the course of our lives. This shift concerns positive thinking and a resilient approach to challenges and opportunities.

Like Yusri Mardini, adapting to adversity can help you see setbacks and failures not as roadblocks but as stepping stones toward greatness. We can learn a lot from different people that have experienced struggles and setbacks their entire life and we can draw inspiration from individuals who've transformed their weaknesses into strengths, such as Stephen Hawking and discover that the triumph of overcoming struggles contributes significantly to our personal growth.

Of course, personal growth requires conquering self-doubt and harnessing the power of self-belief. When we make that internal realization, we can consciously express it by changing on the outside, making it easier to be our most authentic selves.

In conclusion, this journey from 'good' to 'great' is not just about individual success but also about nurturing meaningful relationships, creating shared experiences, and cultivating genuine bonds with loved ones.

Ultimately, the pursuit of passion, aligned with our core values, leads to true happiness and an ongoing journey of life to find triumph in the face of challenges and cherish the moments that define our unique path to greatness.

> "The impact of words cannot be overstated,
> especially in our relationships.
> Words can uplift, inspire, and encourage our
> loved ones." – Peter Bradford

# Final Ode

Abandoning the generic *"I'm good"* for *"Great!"* and the *"Fine"* for *"Buzzing"* has been the smallest decision I've taken that yielded the most outstanding results. When I introduced the concept to my family and friends, seeing their paths to transformation was fascinating. But most of all, I'm proud to see how much it has inspired my daughter, Emma, to realize how limitless she is and how she consistently allows positivity to triumph in her life.

I'm also grateful to Lynette Sharp for so quickly imbibing the spirit of the BeeBetter Movement and coming with me on this journey to get the word out there as a gift to the world. I hope you, dear reader, through discovering your buzzword, realize your potential to be great and live it daily.

But this is not the end; it's merely a pause in our voyage. As you turn the final pages of this chapter, remember that the journey continues. "One Word To BeeBetter" is only the first volume in a series of explorations into the depths of personal transformation. In the following books, we will delve even deeper into how your word choices can subtly affect your relationship, help you understand your purpose, and positively embrace change.

These upcoming volumes will further help you on the path to enlightenment, with each chapter unveiling a new word, a new concept, and a new opportunity to *BeeBetter*. I invite you to embark on this journey with us, exploring new and unfamiliar territories.

Along the way, we'll be guided by the stories and wisdom of individuals who demonstrate the incredible potential of becoming your best self. As you conclude this final chapter and hopefully begin to use the lessons you've learned, remember that every transformation starts with a single word that holds the power to redefine, rebuild, and renew. We become beacons of our best selves through consistent use, living fulfilling lives, setting examples for others, and leaving a meaningful legacy.

This book is our gift to the world. What is your gift? Share it with the world by living it daily, just like we do here in The BeeBetter Movement. And always remember, you are more than you think you are, so think better! So, let us embrace the power of transformation and discover the limitless potential that awaits when we dare to change just one word.

> "And always remember, you are more than you think you are, so think better!" – Peter Bradford

Hi there, dear readers!

I'm so grateful that you decided to purchase my book "One Word to BeeBetter". I hope you enjoyed reading it as much as I enjoyed writing it. This book is a collection of personal experiences and stores that have inspired me to improve myself and my life. I hope they can do the same for you. Thank you for your support and encouragement. You are awesome! So BeeAwesome!

Peter Bradford

www.ingramcontent.com/pod-product-compliance
Lightning Source LLC
Chambersburg PA
CBHW060936180426
43194CB00047B/2879